At Issue

Campus Sexual Violence

Other Books in the At Issue Series:

At Issue

| Campus Sexual
| Violence

Elizabeth Schmermund, Book Editor

GREENHAVEN
PUBLISHING

Published in 2017 by Greenhaven Publishing, LLC
353 3rd Avenue, Suite 255, New York, NY 10010

First Edition

Articles in Greenhaven Publishing anthologies are often edited for length to meet page
requirements. In addition, original titles of these works are changed to clearly present
the main thesis and to explicitly indicate the author's opinion. Every effort is made to
ensure that Greenhaven Publishing accurately reflects the original intent of the authors.
Every effort has been made to trace the owners of the copyrighted material.

Cover image: Polonez/Shutterstock.com

Library of Congress Cataloging-in-Publication Data

Names: Schmermund, Elizabeth.
Title: Campus sexual violence / Elizabeth Schmermund.
Description: New York : Greenhaven Publishing, 2017. | Series: At issue | Includes index.
Identifiers: LCCN ISBN 9781534500372 (pbk.) | ISBN 9781534500181 (library bound)
Subjects: LCSH: Campus violence—United States. | Campus violence—
United States—Prevention. | Sex crimes—United States—Prevention.
| College students—Crimes against—United States.
Classification: LCC LB2345.S34 2017 | DDC 371.7'82—dc23

Manufactured in the United States of America

Website: http://greenhavenpublishing.com

Contents

Introduction

C ampus sexual violence is a very real problem, although there are many differing views about its prevalence, its causes, and the most effective ways of preventing it from occurring. What we do know for sure is that campus sexual violence affects many more women than men, that women may feel shame or fear in reporting a sexual attack that they experienced, and that many universities have historically tried to dissuade victims from contacting the police or going public with information about their attack. Sometimes it is the school's policy that women must confront their attacker without a lawyer present, which is psychologically painful and legally dubious. Many women who have experienced sexual violence on campus feel doubly betrayed: first by their attackers and then by the school officials or local authorities who do not adequately protect their rights.

One of the reasons why sexual violence is a hotly debated topic is because it often devolves into a case of "he said, she said" in courtrooms. If there exists physical evidence of some kind of sexual intimacy, the accused can say that the accused gave her consent. The accuser, of course, disagrees.

The charge of sexual violence is an extremely serious one and can ruin lives; oftentimes, those convicted of sexual crimes must register as a sexual offender for the rest of their lives. While many of those who write on the subject of sexual violence state that, in the US justice system, one is innocent until proven guilty, it is also important not to place the burden of proof on the victim. Oftentimes, women who report sexual assault on campuses are questioned about their lifestyles, their clothing, and whether or not they consumed drugs or alcohol at a party before the attack.

In a well-known case of campus sexual assault in 2015, Brock Turner attacked a woman while she was unconscious following a party at Stanford University. Due to overpowering evidence, Turner was convicted and prosecutors recommended a six-year prison sentence. The judge, Aaron Persky, stunned many with his leniency toward Turner, sentencing him to only six months in the county jail. (Turner was released after serving only three months.) Before sentencing, however, the woman read a powerful victim impact statement that was widely shared in the media. She recounted how school officials and the police questioned her, putting minute details about her life under a microscope: "Did you drink in college? You said you were a party animal? How many times did you black out? Did you party at frats? Are you serious with your boyfriend? Are you sexually active with him?" These questions insinuate that there is a "wrong" answer that will prove that the sexual assault victim was "asking for it." With cases such as this one in the news, is it any surprise that many women choose not to report experiences of sexual violence?

The question of how to protect the rights of victims of sexual violence while still holding that the accuser is innocent until proven guilty is a difficult—if not seemingly impossible— task. But it can and must be done. School officials must actively investigate accusations and not bury any reports of sexual violence on campus that might tarnish the school's reputation. The police must investigate cases of sexual violence as they would any other crime scene. In the past, rape kits have been known to disappear, to be mishandled, or even to be forgotten. The lives of sexual assault victims must not be dissected in court; their behavior before the attack or what they wear is irrelevant to the crime that has taken place.

Perhaps just as important is the now political buzzword "consent." Many feminist critics argue that sexual assault against women (and particularly young women on campuses) is due to the prevalence of "rape culture," in which women are objectified in the media, viewed solely through the lens of the sexual pleasure they can provide men, and instances of sexual violence are largely condoned. The only way to fight against rape culture is to change accepted notions of femininity and masculinity in our culture. This is a job for parents, guardians, and educators as they teach younger generations. Women must be taught that their bodies do not exist solely for the pleasure of the men around them and that they have the right and responsibility to say "no" when they do not want to engage sexually. But men need to be taught what consent means from an early age. Consent means that a woman needs to give permission, either expressly or through her body language, for any sexual encounter to occur—even kissing. A woman can say "no," but she can also freeze up, draw back, or start crying. All of these forms of body language also mean "no." This means that if a woman is too tired, drunk, or sick to give permission, then consent *cannot* occur. According to the Fearless Collective, an advocacy group fighting against sexual violence, men must recognize that they are "more than [their] desire" while women must recognize that they are "more than [their] body."

This seems like a simple solution. However, as you'll see in the selections chosen for this book, practical applications are not always so simple. There are debates over whether statistics that state that one in four women experience sexual assault on campus, over whether rape culture in fact exists, over whether alcohol should be viewed as an important factor in rapes and whether this is an excuse for criminal behavior on the part of sexual attackers. These texts will certainly aid you to think deeper about the topic and consider what your own beliefs might be. However, please remember while you read that one thing is not debatable: sexual violence on campus is a very real problem and one that has not been fully dealt with by many universities. To some extent, debating about statistics is only of secondary or even tertiary concern. The real concern should be preventing these attacks from occurring in the first place. After the fact, it is important to avoid re-traumatizing victims who have been sexually assaulted and to protect their rights. It is also important to guarantee a fair trial to the accused, although, in recent history, those found guilty of sexual assault have been given scandalously lenient sentences.

For those of you who have been victims of sexual violence, please know that there is help and support for you as you navigate this traumatic experience. Organizations that you can reach out to for legal and mental health purposes are listed at the back of the book. As the survivor of Brock Turner's assault wrote, "[T]o girls everywhere, I am with you. On nights when you feel alone, I am with you. When people doubt you or dismiss you, I am with you. I fought everyday for you. So never stop fighting."

1

It's Faulty Institutional Policies, Not Rape Culture, That Endangers Students to Sexual Violence

B. Richardson and J. Shields

Bradford Richardson graduated from Claremont McKenna College with a degree in philosophy, politics, and economics. His cowriter, Professor Jon A. Shields, teaches government at Claremont McKenna College.

Originally published in the politically conservative Commentary *magazine, this article examines the role of alcohol and low university administration oversight in college sexual assault. Arguing that rape culture cannot account for the high incidence of sexual violence on campuses, the authors use data to show that fewer sexual assaults take place on conservative campuses that have "dry" policies and strict visitation guidelines that separate the sexes in dorm rooms. If incidents of sexual assault are higher on campus than off, the authors state, it is the fault of institutions that do not put more social regulations into place, allowing students to enter into a sexually permissive zone straight from the more regulated spaces of their parents' homes.*

T he policy conflict over allegations of sexual assault on college campuses has become a battle over rights. Conservatives worry about the rights of the accused in the hands of overzealous administrators, while liberals fear that those same officials might

"The Real Sexual Assault Problem—and How to Fix It," by B. Richardson and J. Shields, October 1, 2015. Reprinted by permission..

ignore the rights of victims by focusing on due process and thereby adding to the trauma of those who say they were assaulted. In broad legal terms, conservatives say that evidence against the accused should be "clear and convincing," while liberals favor a less demanding standard. This conflict is driven by radically different views of the rape problem itself. Conservatives are concerned that scarred and angry women might be leveling assault charges in the regretful wake of drunken hook-ups, while liberals insist that in such encounters, consent is rarely if ever actually granted.

While such disputes have dominated the discussion, comparatively little attention has been given to a more fundamental question: How can universities lessen the need for these painful trials by reducing sexual exploitation and drunken couplings? Even when reformers think about policies to address the deeper problem, they nearly always neglect social regulations, especially controls on alcohol and dorm life. The University of California, for example, established a task force on sexual assault that "specifically recommended separating the issue of sexual assault from alcohol-awareness education," the *Los Angeles Times* reported. As for co-ed dorm life, the pundit Matthew Yglesias captured the prevailing wisdom when he criticized single-sex dorms, noting that a college student is an "adult, a person fully equipped to enjoy having sex—a fun, affordable, and ecologically sustainable pastime."

Any successful approach to reducing sexual assault on campus will require the reconsideration of these very notions. We have completed a study of more than 1,300 colleges and universities and have found that far fewer accusations of sexual assault are levied at the schools that ban alcohol and prohibit opposite-sex overnight guests in residence halls. Our findings suggest that students are not so much victims of a "rape culture" as they are victims of faulty institutional policies that contribute to a higher risk of sexual assault.

The Campus Study

First, a brief description of our method. We collected data on every college in the *U.S. News and World Report: 2015* rankings that maintains undergraduate dorms. For each college, we calculated the number of reported campus sexual assaults for every 1,000 female students living in its residence halls. We considered only *on-campus* assaults because our goal was to measure the effectiveness of campus social regulations in deterring them. In looking at the effect of alcohol policies, we gathered data from *U.S. News and World Report* as well as from individual college handbooks and websites. We classified campuses as "dry" if they prohibit *all* alcohol possession, consumption, and distribution on campus. Finally, using data from student handbooks and residence-life websites, we divided dorm-visitation policies into two types: Those that banned opposite-sex overnight guests outright, and those that permitted the practice, at least on some days or in some undergraduate dorms.

Here is what we found: In recent years, assault rates have been *3.1 to 4.4 times higher* at the most permissive colleges and universities than at their more restrictive counterparts (see Table 1). That difference is substantial.

Table 1: Assault Rates (per 1000 women) by Campus Characteristics

	2011	2012	2013	CHANGE
Guest ban & dry	0.85	1.15	1.02	+20%
Guest ban only	1.50	1.83	2.21	+47%
Dry only	2.08	2.60	2.74	+32%
No prohibitions	3.07	3.53	4.51	+47%

Consider two campuses—one permissive, the other restrictive—that both house 3,000 female undergraduates in their residence halls. The permissive campus is likely to receive somewhere between 65 and 100 more reports of sexual assault over a 10-year period.

One possible objection to our findings might be that these differences reflect underreporting of sexual assaults at conservative and religious colleges. But while it is true that such underreporting has been an issue on college campuses generally, there is no systematic evidence to suggest a plague of it at conservative or religious campuses in particular. In fact, our evidence shows that reports of sexual assault have been climbing at *all types* of colleges, including at regulated and religious ones (see Tables 1 and 2). The fact that reports have increased everywhere suggests that colleges of all stripes and the students enrolled in them are responding to the heightened national awareness about sexual assault.

Table 2: Assault Rates (per 1000 women) at Religious and Secular Colleges

	2011	2012	2013	CHANGE
Religious colleges	1.52	1.82	2.07	+35%
Secular colleges	2.50	3.07	3.55	+42%

Other studies support this conclusion. A 2009 study by the Center for Public Integrity profiled many permissive colleges with serious underreporting problems, including the University of Colorado, Eastern Michigan University, Florida State, West Virginia University, and Yale. And a 2002 Justice Department study on reporting profiled eight campuses, including two with restrictive social policies: West Virginia State University (dry) and Oklahoma State University (guest ban). While the Justice Department study praised these two colleges for the way they reported and adjudicated cases of sexual assault, it was critical of some of the permissive colleges it profiled. The study, for example, found that the reporting protocols at no-prohibitions UCLA "need[ed] to be tighter in terms of capturing all...cases of rape and sexual assault."

Nonetheless, the same Justice Department suggested that dry policies might actually depress the number of assault reports. "If student victims know that they are in violation of a policy forbidding the use of drugs or alcohol," the study read, "this might make them fearful to report a sexual assault." Its own subsequent research undermined this conjecture. A 2007 DOJ study found that victims who had been incapacitated by drugs or alcohol were much less likely to report assaults, often because they did not consider their memory of the incident good enough to offer a credible report or because they were unsure about whether a crime occurred. Logically, then, the problem of unreported assaults may be especially acute at campuses that do a poor job of controlling alcohol consumption.

It is fair to wonder whether the apparent effects of social regulations are actually driven by religiosity. If they are, it would mean that religion both causes schools to implement these social regulations *and* depresses sexual violence. It is certainly true that religious colleges and universities are much more likely than secular ones to ban alcohol and overnight guests of the opposite sex. It is also true that assault rates are generally lower at religious colleges. But the profession or practice of religion itself does not appear to diminish violence very much. As Table 3 makes clear, permissive

Table 3: Assault Rates (per 1000 women) by Social Regulation at Religious and Secular Colleges

	2011	2012	2013
Secular Colleges			
Guest ban & dry	1.33	1.64	1.76
Guest ban only	1.02	1.52	2.23
Dry only	2.34	2.94	2.23
No prohibitions	2.99	3.50	4.51
Religious Colleges			
Guest ban & dry	0.68	0.99	0.76
Guest ban only	1.67	1.94	2.21
Dry only	0.85	0.98	2.16
No prohibitions	3.34	3.64	4.50

religious and secular colleges suffer from comparatively high levels of sexual assault. And when we assessed the unique influence of religion by including it in a regression analysis with variables for alcohol and guest bans, it had little influence on assault rates and was not statistically significant.

The evidence clearly suggests that secular institutions can control sexual assault without having to "find religion." Indeed, many are doing just that. In our data, 171 secular colleges ban alcohol, 43 ban overnight guests, and 90 do both. The most restrictive secular colleges, moreover, have sexual-assault rates that are 1.7 to 2.8 times lower than those at the most permissive secular schools. Restrictive secular colleges tend to be located in states with conservative values, especially in the Midwest and the Deep South. But given the effectiveness of these regulations at controlling sexual assault, they might appeal to the citizens of deep-blue states as well, especially in this age of "helicopter" parents.

Other factors may influence the efficacy of social regulations. For example, bans on alcohol and overnight guests are unevenly enforced. But since we could only identify the policies themselves, we have no good measure of enforcement. In addition, all overnight bans are not equal. Some campuses, for example, ban opposite-sex guests after 11 p.m., while others allow them in the dorms until 3 a.m. Others still, especially conservative Protestant ones, forbid opposite-sex guests inside dorm rooms at any time of the day or night. Though we did not systematically study such campuses, sexual assault seems to occur rarely in their residence halls. We therefore believe that rates of sexual assault fall lower still when campuses embrace more stringent bans and enforce their own policies.

Why Social Regulations Work

Although our study offers the first quantifiable analysis of campus policies in relation to sexual assault, a large body of research supports its findings. We know, for example, that there is a strong link between sexual assault and alcohol, especially on college campuses. A 2004 study of college students in the *Journal of Studies on Alcohol* found that 72 percent of victims were intoxicated at the time of the assault. Research also shows that young men use alcohol to soften women's reluctance to engage in sex. A 1985 study in the *Archives of Sexual Behavior* found that some 76 percent of college rapists admitted to using alcohol to weaken their victims.

It is not surprising that such men turn to alcohol. The sociologists Mark Regnerus and Jeremy Uecker say that regular alcohol consumption dramatically increases young women's willingness to engage in casual sex. "It's almost as if most students—especially but not only women—have a visceral aversion to casual sex that is only overcome with the help of alcohol," Regnerus and Uecker concluded. This association is not lost on some young men. As one male freshman chillingly informed Regnerus and Uecker, sex under the influence "happens all the time...they'll [the women] regret it, but it's not like a tragedy."

Even when alcohol is not used strategically, its consumption can lead women and men to misinterpret social cues. While alcohol depresses women's ability to assess risk, it diminishes men's ability to accurately perceive women's interest in having sex with them. Alcohol also excites more aggressive and antisocial behavior in men. In a review of the literature, published in 2004 in *Aggression and Violent Behavior*, Antonia Abbey and her colleagues noted: "The cues that usually inhibit sexually aggressive behavior, such as concern about future consequences, sense of morality, or empathy for the victim are likely to be less salient than feelings of anger, frustration, sexual arousal, and entitlement."

Less alcohol, naturally, is consumed on dry campuses. Evidence from a 1994 study of 140 campuses published in JAMA suggests that "individual binge drinking is less likely...if [the school] prohibits alcohol use for all persons (even those older than 21) on campus." Are these differences caused by self-selection rather than by alcohol policies—or in other words, are dry campuses simply more appealing to students less likely to binge-drink? A 2001 study in the *Journal of Studies on Alcohol* suggests that self-selection only partly explains the lower rates of drinking on dry campuses. Drawing on a survey of more than 11,000 students at 19 dry and 76 regular colleges, it found that students who were heavy alcohol drinkers in high school tended to drink less heavily when they attended colleges with dry policies. The same study also undermined the theory that dry policies simply push drinking off campus. It found that on-campus residents at dry colleges were less likely to drink heavily at off-campus events, such as fraternity parties. In fact, the report concluded, "these findings do not support the assumption that displacement of heavy drinking off-campus and a heightened risk of drinking and driving and other drug use will occur at schools that ban alcohol."

Our study found, nonetheless, that dry policies by themselves reduce the sexual-assault rate only modestly, though how much this finding is due to uneven enforcement is hard to say. The 2001 survey noted that while reports of unwanted sexual advances and assaults were less common on dry campuses, the differences were modest. Thus, dry policies seem to work best when they are combined with other regulations, especially bans on overnight guests.

Visitation policies are especially important for two likely reasons. First, they are almost certainly easier to enforce than alcohol bans (since it is much more difficult to conceal persons than, say, bottles). Second, visitation policies target the social settings in which so many campus assaults occur. A 2000 study by the Bureau of Justice Statistics found that approximately 90 percent of on-campus rapes occur in the room of either the victim or the assailant. It further found that half of all campus assaults happen *after* midnight, when students are more likely to be inebriated. Other studies find an even higher incidence of late-night assaults. A 2007 Department of Justice study of more than 5,000 undergraduate women found that 72 percent of assaults occurred after midnight, while some 90 percent of women who were incapacitated by drugs or alcohol reported late-night assaults. It seems, therefore, that visitation restrictions function to separate the sexes *before* they become too drunk to exhibit clear volition and good judgment.

If separating the sexes lowers assault rates, we should also expect fewer reports at single-sex colleges. And that is precisely what we found (see Table 4). Average assault rates are many times lower at single-sex colleges than in co-ed colleges. Nonetheless, social regulations still seem to make a big difference at single-sex colleges.

Table 4: Assault Rates (per 1000 women) at Single-sex and Co-ed Colleges

	2011	2013	2013
Single-sex colleges	0.48	0.91	0.83
Co-ed colleges	2.14	2.60	2.99

Why the Alternatives Fail Us

Despite the possible benefits of bans on alcohol and overnight guests, those who have dedicated their careers to cracking down on sexual assault prefer other remedies. That is why many universities are shifting the burden of proof from victims to perpetrators by lowering evidentiary standards. Making punishment a somewhat more likely consequence of assault may lower its incidence. But given the choice between limiting a student's social freedom or depriving a student his due-process rights, the former is preferable. Those who are examining and policing assault on campus also argue for more education on sexual misconduct. While such efforts might be worthwhile, they are far less likely to protect young women and men as effectively as bans on alcohol and overnight guests.

Why? Because such sobering lessons, even well received, can get lost in the haze and confusion of intoxication, and because every college population is laced with antisocial men who never pay much heed to lessons in empathy. As a large body of research shows, rapists tend to be impulsive and exhibit high levels of narcissism. Such characteristics are found in not only the hardened and poorly educated class of rapists in prisons—but also in the well-educated offenders in our universities. A 1997 study published in *Aggression and Violent Behavior*, for example, found that college rapists possessed much *higher* levels of psychopathic traits than their nonviolent student peers. Another study, published in 1994 in the *Journal of Social and Clinical Psychology*, asked college men to listen to an audiotape of a date rape. Students who had committed sexual assault were much more aroused by the tape than those with no history of violence.

Such men need to be controlled, and it cannot be done through moral suasion. Even the best education campaign cannot inoculate a whole population from crime. Instead, we need to change a social context that is currently tailored to the preferences of those with psychopathic tendencies.

The emphasis on "rape culture" cannot account for the lower incidence of sexual assault on the most conservative and religious campuses where feminist sensibilities are weakest. Such campuses are better at controlling crime, not because they are any more likely to condemn rape and certainly not because they are more progressive, but primarily because they are more regulated social environments.

Progressives who worry about the coercive nature of these regulations should remember that they still grant considerable freedom. Limiting visiting hours, for example, allows plenty of opportunities for sexual intimacy. Established couples can arrange their lives to take advantage of those ample opportunities, just as they are already accustomed to doing. And given how little time the average student spends studying outside the classroom, there is no shortage of hours in the college day for such encounters. Bans on overnight guests are more likely to frustrate drunken hook-ups at 3 a.m. than stifle the sex lives of caring couples.

The deeper problem with social regulations has to do with their limits, not their coerciveness. Most assaults, after all, do happen *off* campus, beyond the easy reach of college social regulations. It is possible, however, that even the off-campus problem could be partially mitigated by on-campus regulations in at least two respects. First, more social order might help students cultivate temperate habits while they are still adjusting to their new freedoms as freshman and sophomores. The 2007 Department of Justice study found that "women who are victimized during college are most likely to be victimized early on in their college tenure," before they have had much experience navigating their new freedoms. Ordered campuses give them time to do so.

Second, colleges could also experiment with curfews in their residence halls, which would help prevent new students from venturing into the late-night party scene off campus. But even if the off-campus problem proves intractable, social regulations can make a significant difference at many schools, especially residential liberal-arts colleges where practically all students live on campus. If these colleges solve their on-campus problem, they solve the problem entirely. On the other hand, student resistance to new social regulations may undermine their effectiveness. If so, new rules may need to be phased in and accompanied by a public-education campaign.

Some conservatives, meanwhile, make a different objection to new regulations: They say that much of what we call assault is mostly the result of drunken hook-ups. In this view, the campaign against sexual assault is a moral panic, fueled by an ideological faith in a mythical problem. But even if conservatives are correct, social regulations should limit these soul-crushing hook-ups, not to mention the false charges and painful trials they can create. As conservatives often emphasize, universities should show more concern for the souls of their students.

Unfortunately, our best universities and colleges have shown little interest in dampening the sexual revolution, at least not until someone yells "rape." As Heather Mac Donald reported recently, Brown University's student services works to help students integrate sex toys into their relationships, including whips and restraints. Tufts University's sex fair, meanwhile, includes dental-dam slingshots and "dildo ring toss," while NYU offers orgasm workshops.

These liberationist campaigns forget that students are still moving into adulthood and have not gotten there yet. Colleges should recognize this transitional period by providing a more structured and less sexualized space for young people to grow into their new freedoms.

Even if our study's findings are confirmed by further research, most campuses may reasonably decide to strike some balance between sexual liberty and security. Few want to follow the lead of fundamentalist colleges by banning any opposite-sex visitation in campus dorm rooms, even though doing so would greatly reduce the risk of assaults in their residence halls. But rejecting the most draconian policies does not mean that *no balance* could or should be struck. Campuses with comparatively high rates of sexual assault must decide whether they are willing to place some modest restrictions on their students, or whether their many rape charges are the necessary price of the sexual revolution.

2

Rape Culture Is Prevalent Both On and Off Campus

Kristen N. Jozkowski

Kristen N. Jozkowski is an assistant professor of public health and a faculty member in gender studies at the University of Arkansas. She specializes in sexual-violence prevention and mutual consent among college students.

In this article, Kristen N. Jozkowski takes up the second-wave feminist motto of "the public is private" to argue that "eruptions" of sexism and rape culture in daily life are what provide the basis for sexual violence on campus. Jozkowski argues for a two-pronged approach: while campus administrations need to more effectively tackle cases of sexual assault, campus culture itself needs to change. This means that everyone on campus—from individual students, to campus groups, to the academic administration, athletic directors, and coaches— needs to decide to come together and change a culture that condones sexual violence against women.

In Short

- California's "Yes Means Yes" legislation—while a notable attempt to address the rape culture prevalent on many campuses—does not take into account how consent is actually negotiated in sexual relations.
- College women are given more permission to be direct in saying no to sex than in saying yes. But some men realize

"'Yes Means Yes?' Sexual Consent Policy and College Students," **by** Kristen N. Jozkowski, Taylor & Francis Group, March-April 2015. Reprinted by permission.

that their partners might not willingly consent to sexual activity, so they avoid a refusal by not asking.

- When women are not aggressive in rejecting sex, campus discourse may suggest that they did not do enough to prevent the assault. This can lead to internalized self-blame, prevent reporting, and perpetuate rape culture.
- Campus climate needs to change. While students need to be involved in this shift, campus administrators, athletic directors and coaches, faculty and staff, and inter-fraternity and PanHellenic councils need to take the lead.
- Those who sit on committees that hear cases of sexual assault need to be properly trained and educated; sexual-assault-prevention initiatives also need to be given adequate resources, and their programs should be made mandatory for all students.
- When not just sexual assaults but egregious eruptions of sexism and rape culture surface, those responsible for them need to be held accountable.

In the past year, some important initiatives have begun to address sexual violence on college campuses and to define sexual consent for college students. For example, in April 2014 the White House Task Force to Protect Students from Sexual Assault released *Not Alone*, a report addressing sexual violence in college and providing recommendations for how to address it.

Title IX of the Education Amendments of 1972 prohibits gender-based discrimination in education programs or associated activities for universities that receive federal financial assistance. Acts of sexual violence, including sexual assault and sexual harassment, are considered forms of discrimination prohibited by Title IX: "If a school knows or reasonably should know about student-on-student harassment that creates a hostile environment, Title IX requires the school to take immediate action to eliminate the harassment, prevent its recurrence, and address its effects" (United States Department of Education's Letter from Secretary of the Office for Civil Rights, p. 4).

Following the establishment of the Task Force and in an effort to increase transparency regarding sexual violence on college campuses, in 2014 the United States Department of Education released a list of institutions under investigation for mishandling or inappropriately handing cases of sexual violence in accordance with Title IX. The list, which started out with 55 campuses in May 2014, now includes over 85.

In light of the increased publicity regarding sexual violence on college campuses generated by the list, universities are beginning to examine their sexual-assault policies, and some are implementing more programming to address the problem. At the same time, some universities have experienced an increase in the number of reported incidents of sexual assault. Awareness-promoting campaigns to address sexual assault may have given students a better understanding of what sexual assault, rape, and consent look like—they often do not include a weapon, are not characterized by extreme violence, and are often perpetrated by someone known to the victim.

For example, the University of Connecticut's reports of sexual assault nearly doubled from 2012 to 2013. The local police attributed the steep increase in these reports to heightened awareness of sexual violence in general and to women's better recognizing their experiences of nonconsensual sex as "rape" or "sexual assault" (Megan, 2014). Other universities have acknowledged similar trends.

Sexual assault and consent have also captured the attention of policymakers. In September 2014, California passed legislation that directed the state's public institutions of higher education to implement an affirmative-consent (i.e., "yes means yes") policy in regard to sexual encounters among students. According to this legislation, students need to not only verbally agree to engage in sexual activity initially, but the parties involved need to explicitly say yes to one another for each sexual behavior they engage in as part of a sexual interaction.

On the surface, this seems like a policy that could help address problems of sexual violence on college campuses by increasing communication about agreements to engage in sex. But critics question the law for a variety of reasons.

Some believe that by dictating how to negotiate sex, the government is infringing on people's rights in the bedroom. Others argue that an affirmative-consent policy will not reduce the rates of sexual assault because it does not protect those who are sexually assaulted while under the influence of alcohol (or other drugs). An affirmative-consent policy, critics further believe, will not change the "he said/she said" difficulty in prosecuting sexual assault, since the accused will now simply report that "she said yes" instead of "she didn't say no" (Bogle, 2014).

Finally, there are critics who, while finding some benefit in such a policy, argue that it ignores the larger social context: Sexism, patriarchy, and hegemonic masculinity pervade college campuses, just as they do society as a whole. They contribute to and facilitate sexual violence.

Nevertheless, most sexual-assault researchers and advocates, school administrators, students and parents, policymakers, and the lay public agree that something needs to be done to address sexual assaults on college campuses. Current statistics indicate that one in five women will experience a rape or attempted rape during her lifetime, with increased risk when she is in college (Daigle, Fisher, & Cullen, 2008; Krebs et al., 2007; Tjaden & Thoennes, 2006). The 1970's women's movement can be credited for increasing awareness about sexual violence, but since then, have we made much progress?

Researchers, at least, have made some advances in understanding the rape culture that permeates and profoundly affects consent negotiation. Here I examine some of the messages that culture sends regarding sexual consent and the ways in which it influences the sexual behavior of college students in the United States.

Rape Culture and Sexual Consent

Over the last few years, we have seen some egregious examples of rape culture on college campuses that call into question the effectiveness of current sexual-assault policies. What follows is a brief recap of four recent events that took place at prominent American universities, drawn from a laundry list of contemporary examples. They exemplify rape culture in general, but they specifically demonstrate a deliberate disregard for consent.

Yale University's "No Means Yes, Yes Means Anal" Chant

In 2010, pledges and members of the Delta Kappa Epsilon (DKE) fraternity at Yale University chanted "No means yes and yes means anal" and "My name is Jack, I'm a necrophiliac, I f--- dead women and fill them with my semen" while walking around outside freshmen women's residence halls as part of an alleged hazing ritual. The day after they engaged in this behavior, the DKE president apologized for the incident, calling it "a serious lapse in judgment by the fraternity and in very poor taste."

The fraternity's initial punishment following the event was that five men from the fraternity had to meet with representatives from the Women's Students Office at Yale. The Yale administration's response (or lack thereof) to the incident spurred law suits and garnered media attention, since the university inadequately addressed the gender-based violence inherent in the men's activity (Zeavin, 2010).

University of Southern California's "Gullet Report"

In 2011, a mechanism for tracking the number of women whom men in the Kappa Sigma (KS) fraternity at the University of Southern California (USC) engaged in sexual activity with, called the "gullet report," was brought to the attention of campus administrators and ultimately the mainstream media via an email circulating on the USC campus. The email, allegedly written by a member of KS fraternity, described the purpose of the gullet report as follows: "I want raw data on who f---s and who doesn't. ... The gullet report will strengthen brotherhood and help pin-point sorostitutes more inclined to put-out. … My hope is that ALL of our brothers will follow this creed with pride and distinction."

The long email provided detailed information on how the "brothers" should keep track of the women they engaged in sexual activity with and specific language to use as part of the tracking "game." Until recently, BroBible.com described the report on its website, taking the position that it was not offensive and that those who found it objectionable needed to lighten up. BroBible has since removed the material from its website, but the entire email can still be found at Jezebel.com.

The gullet report awarded points to men based on the number of women they engaged in sexual activity with; they earned more points if the women were perceived to be attractive. In the description of the tracking system, the author wrote, "Note, I will refer to females as 'targets.' They aren't actual people like us men. Consequently, giving them a certain name or distinction is pointless." He then goes on to objectify women further by using words such as "pie" (i.e., vagina) and "gullet" (i.e., mouth) to describe women's body parts, and he names the men playing the "game" "Cocksmen."

Particularly relevant to a discussion about consent was the first of the "Additional Rules for a Cocksman," which was worded as follows: "Non-consent and rape are two different things. There is a fine line, so make sure not to cross it." The message communicated via this rule is that non-consensual sex is something that you can get away with, but rape is not—and as long as you can get away with it, whatever tactics you use to obtain sex are fine, as long as the non-consensual sex (i.e., sexual assault) is not so outrageous or violent that you raise suspicions of rape (Hartman, 2011).

Miami University of Ohio's Top Ten
Ways to Get Away with Rape

Fraternities are the culprits in the two initial examples provided, but they are not alone. In 2012, a flier was posted in the men's restrooms in a co-ed residence hall at Miami University of Ohio that read: "Top Ten Ways to Get Away with Rape." The flier recommended, among other things, the rape of women who are unconscious: "Put drugs in the woman's drink," it counsels—"therefore she won't remember you." The last recommendation read: "Rape, rape, rape!! It's college boys, live it up!!"

The university responded by holding a mandatory meeting for the male students in that residence hall and increasing police presence there. Additionally, the police launched an investigation into who posted the fliers. In 2012, the university's director of news and public information stated that if found, the individual(s) responsible could face repercussions such as being removed from the residence hall, attending mandatory educational programs, or suspension. It is unclear whether the administration and/or the police ever identified the responsible party (Roberts, 2012).

University of Kansas' Sexual Assault

At the University of Kansas, a perpetrator of a 2013 sexual assault who was found guilty by the university received a minor punishment. In this incident, the perpetrator acknowledged that sexual intercourse had occurred without consent. According to him, the victim said, "No," "Stop," and "I can't do this" prior to his forcing sex on her.

Yet he was not expelled, permanently or temporarily, from the university, as long as he agreed to seek counseling. Instead he was ejected from university housing, put on probation, and instructed to write a four-page paper.

This incident received national media attention because of the way the University of Kansas handled it. The chancellor's email to the campus asserted that it was up to the students to protect one another from sexual assault. Additionally, the university's spokespersons avoided the words "sexual assault" to describe the incident, using, instead, the more neutral (if synonymous) term, "non-consensual sex." In doing so, the institution seemed to imply that sex without consent is somehow not sexual assault and that such incidents thus ought not to have severe repercussions (Kingkade, 2014).

These contemporary examples challenge the very notion of what it means to engage in consensual sex. They all emphasize an important theme: *consent does not matter*—a belief that seems to be deeply rooted in the culture of universities and in society as a whole.

In light of California's "yes means yes" policy, this raises an important question: Will an affirmative-consent policy help reduce rates of sexual assault? This question cannot be answered without examining how college students currently negotiate sexual consent.

Contemporary Consent Research

Rape and sexual-assault research is abundant in the peer-reviewed scientific literature. By comparison, there is little research examining sexual consent (Beres, 2007). This is somewhat surprising, given that 1) sexual assault/rape is typically defined as non-consensual sex (Hickman & Muehlenhard, 1999), 2) many sexual-assault-prevention education programs are built around consent promotion (Donat & White, 2000; Schewe, 2006), and 3) consent research could contribute to our understanding of the effects of affirmative-consent policies.

Hall (1998) and Hickman and Muehlenhard (1999) were among the first to examine sexual consent among college students. They presented heterosexual college students with a list of 34 behaviors and vignettes in which individuals engaged in vaginal-penile intercourse. Hickman and Muehlenhard asked the students to read the vignettes and then indicate which of the 34 behaviors they believed the couple in the vignette used to communicate sexual consent. College students identified the non-verbal cues as communicating consent more frequently than they did the verbal ones.

Similarly, Hall (1998) provided students with a list of sexual behaviors and asked if they communicated permission using verbal or non-verbal cues to engage in those behaviors. Like Hickman and Muehlenhard, Hall found that college students more frequently used non-verbal cues to communicate permission.

However, Hall did find differences across sexual behaviors. Students more frequently reported using non-verbal cues to indicate permission for behaviors such as kissing and genital touching. By comparison, they used more verbal cues to indicate permission to engage in sexual intercourse.

More recently, Jozkowski et al. (2013) examined how heterosexual college students indicated consent to a range of sexual behaviors. Their respondents too reported that non-verbal cues were given more frequently for kissing/touching behaviors, whereas verbal cues were used more frequently for intercourse behaviors (vaginal-penile or anal-penile), with oral sex falling in the middle.

Jozkowski et al. examined gender differences in consent cues as well. In their study, men more frequently reported using non-verbal cues to both communicate sexual consent to a partner and interpret consent from that partner. But women in their sample reported more frequent use of verbal cues to communicate consent and reported using verbal, non-verbal, and a combination of cues to interpret consent from a partner.

According to Jozkowski and Peterson (2013), the ways in which college students communicate consent seem to mirror the traditional sexual script, with men acting as sexual initiators and women acting as sexual gatekeepers. Specifically, in Jozkowski and Peterson's study, women's use of verbal cues to communicate consent was consistent with the traditional sexual script: The women reported giving consent by responding verbally to men's requests for sex (Wiederman, 2005). However, if men do not open the dialogue by asking for consent, it is unclear how these women would communicate consent.

Moreover, Jozkowski and Peterson (2013) found that a small percentage of men reported being intentionally deceptive in their approach to consent. About 13 percent of men in their sample stated that they start having sex with their partner and then, if the partner objects, pretend as though they inserted their penis "by mistake."

This finding is worrisome on a number of counts. First, it demonstrates that some men think about consent primarily in terms of how they can obtain sex instead of as a probe for their partner's agreement to or interest in sexual behavior. Second, some of these men seemed to realize that their partners might not willingly consent to sexual activity, so they avoid a refusal by not asking. Finally, if women are waiting to be asked for their consent, as suggested by the traditional sexual script, there is a potential for non-consensual sex to occur if men are "taking without asking."

These findings highlight an important point of contention among sexual-consent/sexual-communication researchers: whether or not men and women miscommunicate consent cues, resulting in sexual assault, or whether they have a shared understanding of those cues.

Miscommunication Theory
Some researchers (e.g., Abbey, 1991; Abbey, McAuslan, & Ross, 1998; Jozkowski et al., 2013; Tannen, 1992) suggest that the differences in how men and women communicate sexual consent can lead to misunderstandings that could result in non-consensual/assaultive sex. This conceptualization of sexual consent has been labeled the "miscommunication theory," since it posits that some sexual assault occurs as a result of misunderstanding or miscommunication regarding sexual consent (Tannen, 1992).

This theory suggests that at least some men either do not understand that they need to obtain consent from their sexual partners or they do not understand what obtaining consent looks like during a sexual encounter. Thus, according to the miscommunication theory, obtaining clear consent via affirmative consent (yes means yes) and understanding strong, assertive refusals (no means no), will prevent sexual assault.

The miscommunication theory provides the foundation for consent-promotion-based campaigns, a dominant model in sexual-assault-prevention education (Crawford, 1995; Donat & White, 2000; Schewe, 2006). If the miscommunication theory is accurate, an affirmative-consent model such as California's "yes means yes" policy may be effective in reducing rates of sexual assault.

Refutations of the Miscommunication Theory

Those who refute the miscommunication theory argue that men and women frequently negotiate consent via subtle, non-verbal cues and in most instances are able to accurately interpret each other's cues (Beres, 2010; Beres, Senn, & McCaw, 2013; Frith & Kitzinger, 1997; McCaw & Senn, 1998; O'Byrne, Hansen, & Rapley, 2008). O'Byrne, Rapley, and Hansen (2006) reported that men accurately understand women's sexual refusals, even those refusals that are communicated in subtle, implicit ways. Similarly, Beres (2010) found that men and women communicated consent via "tacit knowledge"—they know or have a sense of their partner's consent from non-verbal cues and contextual factors associated with the interaction.

Consistent with these findings, Jozkowski and Hunt (2013) found that students in their sample believed they could accurately interpret consent to casual sex (i.e., hooking up) via a progression of subtle non-verbal cues communicated over time, beginning in a social context (e.g., at a bar or party). In fact, the action of transitioning from the bar to a place of residence was frequently identified as a consent cue by young adults and college students (e.g., Beres, 2010; Jozkowski & Hunt, 2013). If we believe that men and women accurately understand each other's consent cues, as suggested by these researchers, then affirmative-consent policies are not likely to have much effect.

But in addition to understanding college students' conceptualizations of consent, it may be helpful to understand the factors that influence consent communication.

Consent Negotiation Norms

In addition to understanding conceptualizations of consent, it is equally important to comprehend gender power dynamics on college campuses and how they influence consent communication by examining *consent* through a gendered lens.

Feminists have discussed gender power dynamics in both the peer-reviewed literature and the mainstream media. Some of the examples of rape culture described above are rooted in gender inequity and a hegemonic masculinity that seems to prevail on many college campuses in the United States.

An underlying factor that influences college students' consent negotiation is our culture's continued constraint of women's sexuality. Nearly five years ago, in a blog post for Kinsey Confidential, I posed the question–can women really say yes to sex? (Jozkowski, 2010). The question remains relevant today. When women say yes to sex "too often" or desire "too much" sex, they may be labeled "sluts" or "whores." Women are aware they run the risk of being categorized in this way and have learned to act accordingly.

For example, in a qualitative study, Hunt and Jozkowski (2014) found that college women reported refusing vaginal-penile sex during a hook up because they did not want to develop a bad reputation. Hamilton and Armstrong (2009) describe how college women who do not want to be in romantic relationships but do want to be sexually active try to avoid negative labels: They stay in relationships they are unhappy with.

So if women are not respected when they say yes to sex they want and agree to, why would their refusals be respected? And although college women are given more permission to be direct in regard to saying no to sex than to saying yes, they are apt to find being explicit in refusing sex problematic.

As they do with other types of refusals, women often refuse sex by first offering some kind of palliative remark, such as expressing appreciation or making an apology (e.g., "That's kind of you, but..."; I'm really flattered but...")—followed by an explanation to justify, excuse, or redefine the rejection (e.g., "It's not you, it's me") (Kitzinger and Frith, 1999). According to Jozkowski and Humphreys (2014),

> the account usually describes their *inability* rather than their *unwillingness* to engage in sexual activity. Rarely do people say no without providing justification for their responses. To do so would seem awkward, rude, arrogant, or even hostile. It violates culturally accepted norms of conversation.

Many college women seem to be worried about hurting men's feelings by being too upfront in their refusals (e.g., Burkett & Hamilton, 2012; Jozkowski & Hunt, 2014), whereas men report expecting and preferring women to be obvious in their sexual refusals (O'Byrne, et al., 2006; 2008). Many men interpret faint refusals as a desire for sex mediated by the desire not to appear sexually "easy" (O'Byrne, et al., 2006; 2008). Thus, there is a consequent potential for miscommunication.

These findings suggest that in order for men to interpret women's refusals as genuine, women have to be blunt, explicit, curt, or aggressive. These traits are not socially acceptable for women in general and certainly buck gender norms in the context of hook ups (Armstrong, Hamilton, & Sweeney, 2006).

But when women are not aggressive in rejecting sex, not only are their partners likely to misunderstand their desires—campus discourse may suggest that they did not do enough to "prevent the assault." This can lead to internalized self-blame, prevent reporting, and perpetuate rape culture. According to Burkett and Hamilton (2012), women should be empowered to say no or yes to sex, but gender imbalances and inequalities exist in college culture that limit women's actual ability to be listened to and respected.

Gender norms are further implicated in the dynamics of relationships and sexual history, both of which, previous research suggests, influence consent negotiation. General relationship norms seem to dictate that sexual behavior, and specifically sexual intercourse, is assumed within intimate relationships (Gavey, McPhillips, & Braun, 1999). So explicit consent in the context of a relationship in which sex has previously occurred may seem unnecessary, because consent is assumed through the acts of previous sexual intercourse.

Empirical data—including 1) accounts from men regarding the degree to which sex is expected once a couple is over the age of 18 and in a relationship (O'Byrne et al., 2008) and 2) college students' interpretations of ambiguous sexual encounters as consensual when the individuals engaged in the sexual activity have had sex previously (Humphreys, 2007)—verify that these norms exist. Burkett and Hamilton (2012) too found that women's perceptions of consent shift based on relationship status. Women in their sample tended to consider uncomfortable or unwanted sex to be a form of "relationship maintenance," as opposed to something they could refuse.

Marital rape laws in the United States have reflected the perception that consent within the context of a romantic relationship (i.e., marriage) is assumed. Prior to the 1970's, marital rape (i.e., forced/nonconsensual sex occurring between individuals who are married) was exempted from rape laws. For example, language used in legislation defined rape as something that occurred between unmarried individuals: "A male who has sexual intercourse with a female not his wife is guilty of rape if…" (*Model Penal Code*, 1962).

In 1984, New York was the first state to consider the marital exemption unconstitutional: "A marriage license should not be viewed as a license for a husband to forcibly rape his wife with impunity. A married woman has the same right to control her own body as does an unmarried woman" (People v. Liberta, 1984). Soon after, other states followed suit and by 1993, all fifty states recognized marital rape. However, even today some states distinguish between marital and non-martial rape.

What Does the Research Imply for a "Yes Means Yes" Policy?

To recap, an affirmative-consent policy rests on the belief that if men and women were more explicit in their consent communication (i.e., by saying yes to sex), there would be reductions in rates of sexual assault. So, given what we know about college students' consent communication, will an affirmative-consent policy be effective?

Such a policy means that if a person asks for consent and his/her partner says yes, both expect that consensual sex will follow (assuming they have a shared understanding of the behaviors they are both asking and agreeing to). In this case, an affirmative policy may be helpful in regard to increasing dialogue between individuals engaged in sex, which could—as proponents of affirmative consent have argued (e.g., Millar, 2008; Jozkowski, 2013)—increase enjoyment in the sexual activity.

However, consider another scenario: A man asks his female partner for consent (hoping she will say yes), but his partner refuses or says nothing at all. The expectation should be that the sexual activity will halt, right? A "yes means yes" policy implies that silence means no. As a statement of human rights, this should certainly be the case.

But saying no without an explanation is conversationally uncommon for women, and absent or non-obvious gestures of refusals are sometimes interpreted by even conscientious men as women's non-verbal cues of consent. Thus, something needs to change in order for affirmative-consent policies to be effective.

Campus climate is that thing that needs to change. While students need to be involved in this shift, those at the top (including campus administrators, athletic directors and coaches, faculty and staff, and inter-fraternity and PanHellenic councils, etc.) need to take the lead. And in order for them to demonstrate a genuine commitment to eliminating sexual assault, strong campus-level policies need to be in place, and violations of those policies need to result in serious repercussions.

Shifting the Campus Climate

Generally speaking, current sexual-assault-prevention initiatives and even contemporary discourse put the onus on women to avoid rape by being more sexually assertive (consent-promotion programming), monitoring their alcohol consumption (risk-reduction programming), having a buddy system to look out for friends who might get assaulted (bystander-intervention programming), etc. Such approaches underscore the importance of personal responsibility on the part of women (and to a smaller extent, bystanders) to prevent sexual assault. At the same time they also deemphasize the role of male perpetrators—especially when the perpetrators are well-known individuals (e.g., star athletes).

Such initiatives and general discourse also focus so intently on individual behaviors that they understate the importance of the sociocultural environment in which the sexual assault occurs. In order to address sexual violence on college campuses, we need to identify the features of rape culture—such as patriarchal ideology and institutions of male dominance and entitlement—that are linked to sexual assault and aggression, and then to change that culture.

Policy can play an important role in doing so. There are countless examples of effective policy-level public-health interventions that have had long-lasting effects. For example, "Click it or Ticket" campaigns have been successful in increasing people's use of seat belts while driving (National Highway Traffic Safety Administration, 2014). Vaccination polices have also worked: They have increased vaccination rates and reduced the rates of or eradicated certain serious diseases.

Finally, smoking-policies exemplify how policy-level interventions can shift cultural norms. In the 1970's, people smoked cigarettes freely in public spaces such as college classrooms and business meetings. When smoking bans were instituted, people were forced to refrain from smoking in those spaces. Fast forward to 2015: Now, a professor who lights up a cigarette while teaching a class would be violating not only campus policy but cultural norms.

If college students are forced, by means of a "yes means yes" policy, to obtain affirmative consent, over time explicitness in consent communication might be adopted as a cultural standard. But for this to happen, affirmative-consent policies need to be championed by campus leaders.

And because of the need for serious repercussions in cases of policy violations, faculty, students, and staff who sit on committees that hear cases of sexual assault need to be properly trained and educated. Moreover, if such individuals engage in victim blaming, they need to be removed from these positions and held accountable.

At the same time, sexual-assault-prevention initiatives need to be given adequate resources, and such programming should be mandatory for all students. This programming should not be limited to one 45-minute session telling women to avoid drinking and walking alone at night; it should be ongoing rather than confined to freshman orientation and include initiatives that highlight gender inequity.

Finally, when egregious eruptions of sexism and rape culture such as "no means yes and yes means anal," and "rape, rape, rape, it's college boys, live it up" surface, those responsible for them, as well as their institutions (e.g., the *entire* fraternity), need to be held accountable. For a "yes means yes" policy to make a difference, it needs to be enacted in a way that addresses rape culture in a serious and meaningful way.

Resources

Abbey, A. (1991). Acquaintance rape and alcohol consumption on college campuses: How are they linked? *Journal of American College Health*, 39, 165–169.

Abbey, A., Ross, L. T., McDuffie, D., & McAuslan, P. (1996). Alcohol and dating risk factors for sexual assault among college women. *Psychology of Women Quarterly*, 20, 147–169.

Armstrong, E. A., Hamilton, L., & Sweeney, B. (2006). Sexual assault on campus: A multilevel integrative approach to party rape. *Social Problems*, 53(4), 483–499.

Beres, M. A. (2007). "Spontaneous" sexual consent: An analysis of sexual consent literature. *Feminism and Psychology*, 17, 93–108. doi:10.1177=0959353507072914

Beres, M. A. (2010). Sexual miscommunication? Untangling assumptions about sexual communication between casual sex partners. *Culture, Health & Sexuality*, 12(1), 1–14.

Beres, M. A., Senn, C. Y., & McCaw, J. (2013). Navigating ambivalence: How heterosexual young adults make sense of desire differences. *Journal of Sex Research*. Online advance of print. doi:10.1080/00224499.2013.792327

Bogle, K.A. (2014, October 27). "Yes means yes" isn't the answer. *The Chronicle of Higher Education*. Retrieved from http://chronicle.com/article/Yes-Means-Yes-Isnt-the/149639/

Burkett, M., & Hamilton, K. (2012). Postfeminist sexual agency: Young women's negotiations of sexual consent. *Sexualities*, 15(7), 815–833.

Crawford, M. (1995). *Talking difference: On gender and language*. London, England: Sage.

Daigle, L.E., Fisher, B.S., & Cullen, F.T. (2008). The violent and sexual victimization of college women: Is repeat victimization a problem? *Journal of Interpersonal Violence*, 23, 1296–1313.

Donat, P. L. N., & White, J. W. (2000). Re-examining the issue of non-consent in acquaintance rape. In C. B. Travis & J. W. White (Eds.), *Sexuality, society, & feminism* (pp. 355–376). Washington, DC: American Psychological Association.

Frith, H., & Kitzinger, C. (1997). Talk about sexual miscommunication. *Women's Studies International Forum*, 20(4), 517–527.

Gavey, N., McPhillips, K., & Braun, V. (1999). Interruptus coitus: Heterosexuals accounting for intercourse. *Sexualities*, 2(1), 35–68.

Hall, D. S. (1998, August 10). Consent for sexual behavior in a college student population. *Electronic Journal of Human Sexuality*, 1. Retrieved from http://www.ejhs.org/tocv1.htm

Hamilton, L., & Armstrong, E. A. (2009). Gendered sexuality in young adulthood: Double binds and flawed options. *Gender & Society*, 23, 589–616.

Hartman, M. (2011, March 8). Frat email explains women are "targets," not "actual people." *Jezebel*. Retrieved from http://

jezebel.com/5779905/usc-frat-guys-email-explains-women-are -targets-not-actual-people-like-us-men

Hickman, S. E., & Muehlenhard, C. L. (1999). "By the semi-mystical appearance of a condom": How young women and men communicate consent in heterosexual situations. *The Journal of Sex Research*, 36, 258–272. doi: 10.1080/00224499909551996

Humphreys, T. P. (2007). Perceptions of sexual consent: The impact of relationship history and gender. *The Journal of Sex Research*, 44(4), 307–315.

Hunt, M., & Jozkowski, K. (2014, November). *"There is nothing to work towards if they are getting it already": Emerging themes in college students' sexual decision-making regarding hooking up.* Paper presentation at the Society for the Scientific Study of Sexuality Conference, Omaha, Nebraska.

Jozkowski, K.N. (2010, August). Can women ever really say yes…? *Kinsey Confident: Sexual Health Information from The Kinsey Institute.* Retrieved from http://kinseyconfidential.org/women/

Jozkowski, K.N. (2013). The influence of consent on college students' perceptions of the quality of sexual intercourse at last event. *International Journal of Sexual Health*, 25, 260–272. doi: 10.1080/19317611.2013.799626

Jozkowski, K.N., & Humphreys, T.P. (2014). Sexual consent on college campuses: Implications for sexual assault prevention education. *Health Education Monograph*, 31(2), 30–36.

Jozkowski, K.N., & Hunt, M. (2013, November). *Beyond the dyad: When does consent to sex begin?* Paper presented at the annual meeting of the Society for the Scientific Study of Sexuality, San Diego, CA.

Jozkowski, K.N., & Hunt, M. (2014, November). '*Who wants a quitter?…So you just keep trying': How college students' perceptions of sexual consent privilege men.* Paper presented at the meeting of the Society for the Scientific Study of Sexuality, Omaha, Nebraska.

Jozkowski, K. N., & Peterson, Z. D. (2013). College students and sexual consent: Unique insights. *Journal of Sex Research*, 50(6), 517–523.

Jozkowski, K. N., Peterson, Z. D., Sanders, S. A., Dennis, B., & Reece, M. (2013). Gender differences in heterosexual college students' conceptualizations and indicators of sexual consent: Implications for contemporary sexual assault prevention education. *Journal of Sex Research*. Online advance of print. doi: 10.1080/00224499.2013.792326

Kingkade, T. (2014, September 4). KU students outraged over soft punishment in rape case. *The Huffington Post*. Retrieved from http://www.huffingtonpost.com/2014/09/04/ku-rape -students_n_5767824.html

Kitzinger, C., & Frith, H. (1999). Just say no? The use of conversation analysis in developing a feminist perspective on sexual refusal. *Discourse and Society*, 10, 293–316.

Krebs, C. P., Lindquist, C.H., Warner, T.D., Fisher, B.S., Martin, S.L. (2007). *The Campus Sexual Assault (CSA) study*. National Institute of Justice. NIJ Grant No. 2004-WG-BX-0010.

McCaw, J. M., & Senn, C. Y. (1998). Perception of cues in conflictual dating situations. *Violence Against Women*, 4, 609–642.

Megan, K. (2014, October 25). Reports of sexual assault on college campuses climb as more victims come forward. *Hartford Courant Education*. Retrieved from http://www.courant.com/education/ hc-clery-campus-sexual-assault-1016-20141025-story .html#page=1

Millar, T.M. (2008). Toward a performance model of sex. In J. Friendman, & J. Valenti (Eds.) *Yes means yes! Visions of female sexual power and a world without rape* (pp. 29–42). Berkeley, CA: Seal.

National Highway Traffic Safety Administration (2014). Don't get fakcd out: Click it or ticket. Retrieved from http://www.nhtsa .gov/nhtsa/ciot/stats.html

O'Byrne, R., Rapley, M., & Hansen, S. (2006). "You couldn't say 'no,' could you?" Young men's understandings of sexual refusal. *Feminism and Psychology*, 16, 133–154.

O'Byrne, R., Hansen, S., & Rapley, M. (2008). "If a girl doesn't say 'no'…": Young men, rape and claims of "insufficient knowledge." *Journal of Community & Applied Social Psychology*, 18, 168–193.

Roberts, C. (2012). Flier found at Miami University in Ohio advises "top ten says to get away with rape."*Daily News*. Retrieved from http://www.nydailynews.com/news/national/flier-found-miami -university-ohio-advises-top-ten-ways-rape-article-1.1184009

Schewe, P.A. (2006). Interventions to prevent sexual violence. In Paul A. Schewe (eds). *Preventing violence in relationships: Interventions across the life span* (pp. 223–239). Washington, DC: American Psychological Association.

Tannen, D. (1992). *You just don't understand: Women and men in conversation.* London, England: Virago.

Tjaden, P., & Thoennes, N. (2006). *Extent, nature, and consequences of rape victimization: Findings from the National Violence Against Women Survey.* Washington, DC: Department of Justice (US); Publication No. NCJ210346.

United States Department of Education: Office for Civil Rights. (2011). *Dear colleague letter: Sexual violence.* Retrieved from http://www2.ed.gov/about/offices/list/ocr/letters/colleague-201104.pdf

White House Task Force to Protect Students From Sexual Assault (US). (2014). *Not alone: The first report of the White House Task Force to Protect Students From Sexual Assault.*

Wiederman, M. W. (2005). The gendered nature of sexual scripts. *Family Journal,* 13, 496–502. doi:10.1177=1066480705278729

Zeavin, H. (2010, October, 14). The last straw: SKE sponsors hate speech on Yale's old campus. *Broad Recognition: A Feminist Magazine at Yale.* Retrieved from http://broadrecognition.com/yale-new-haven/the-straw-that-broke-the-camel%E2%80%99s-back-dke-sponsors-verbal-assault-on-yale%E2%80%99s-old-campus/

3

The Consequence of Sexual Assault Needs to Be Severe Enough to Be Preventative

Emily Doe

The real name of the author, a twenty-two-year-old woman, is unknown to protect her identity. However, she is known under the pseudonym of "Emily Doe."

On January 18, 2015, two students discovered Brock Turner sexually assaulting an unconscious woman ("Emily Doe") behind a dumpster on the Stanford University campus. Turner was apprehended, and so began a long legal process. He was indicted on charges of rape and sexual assault on January 28 and convicted of sexual assault on March 30, 2016. Prior to his sentencing, Doe presented her victim impact statement before the court. In it, she expressed the damage of the assault and the ensuing investigation on her life, and especially her physical and mental health. She accuses the police of putting her life unfairly under investigation, the media for condoning Turner's behavior due to his status as a well known Stanford athlete, and Turner, himself, not only for his crime but for his lack of repentance. This is an excerpt from that victim impact statement.

Your honor,

If it is all right, for the majority of this statement I would like to address the defendant directly.

You don't know me, but you've been inside me, and that's why we're here today.

Source: Anonymous, Victim Statement to the Judge in Stanford Rape Case, Santa Clara County, California.

On January 17th, 2015, it was a quiet Saturday night at home. My dad made some dinner and I sat at the table with my younger sister who was visiting for the weekend. I was working full time and it was approaching my bed time. I planned to stay at home by myself, watch some TV and read, while she went to a party with her friends. Then, I decided it was my only night with her, I had nothing better to do, so why not, there's a dumb party ten minutes from my house, I would go, dance weird like a fool, and embarrass my younger sister. On the way there, I joked that undergrad guys would have braces. My sister teased me for wearing a beige cardigan to a frat party like a librarian. I called myself "big mama," because I knew I'd be the oldest one there. I made silly faces, let my guard down, and drank liquor too fast not factoring in that my tolerance had significantly lowered since college.

The next thing I remember I was in a gurney in a hallway. I had dried blood and bandages on the backs of my hands and elbow. I thought maybe I had fallen and was in an admin office on campus. I was very calm and wondering where my sister was. A deputy explained I had been assaulted. I still remained calm, assured he was speaking to the wrong person. I knew no one at this party. When I was finally allowed to use the restroom, I pulled down the hospital pants they had given me, went to pull down my underwear, and felt nothing. I still remember the feeling of my hands touching my skin and grabbing nothing. I looked down and there was nothing. The thin piece of fabric, the only thing between my vagina and anything else, was missing and everything inside me was silenced. I still don't have words for that feeling. In order to keep breathing, I thought maybe the policemen used scissors to cut them off for evidence.

Then, I felt pine needles scratching the back of my neck and started pulling them out my hair. I thought maybe, the pine needles had fallen from a tree onto my head. My brain was talking my gut into not collapsing. Because my gut was saying, help me, help me.

I shuffled from room to room with a blanket wrapped around me, pine needles trailing behind me, I left a little pile in every room I sat in. I was asked to sign papers that said "Rape Victim" and I thought something has really happened. My clothes were confiscated and I stood naked while the nurses held a ruler to various abrasions on my body and photographed them. The three of us worked to comb the pine needles out of my hair, six hands to fill one paper bag. To calm me down, they said it's just the flora and fauna, flora and fauna. I had multiple swabs inserted into my vagina and anus, needles for shots, pills, had a nikon pointed right into my spread legs. I had long, pointed beaks inside me and had my vagina smeared with cold, blue paint to check for abrasions.

After a few hours of this, they let me shower. I stood there examining my body beneath the stream of water and decided, I don't want my body anymore. I was terrified of it, I didn't know what had been in it, if it had been contaminated, who had touched it. I wanted to take off my body like a jacket and leave it at the hospital with everything else.

On that morning, all that I was told was that I had been found behind a dumpster, potentially penetrated by a stranger, and that I should get retested for HIV because results don't always show up immediately. But for now, I should go home and get back to my normal life. Imagine stepping back into the world with only that information. They gave me huge hugs, and then I walked out of the hospital into the parking lot wearing the new sweatshirt and sweatpants they provided me, as they had only allowed me to keep my necklace and shoes.

My sister picked me up, face wet from tears and contorted in anguish. Instinctively and immediately, I wanted to take away her pain. I smiled at her, I told her to look at me, I'm right here, I'm okay, everything's okay, I'm right here. My hair is washed and clean, they gave me the strangest shampoo, calm down, and look at me. Look at these funny new sweatpants and sweatshirt, I look like a P.E. teacher, let's go home, let's eat something. She did not know that beneath my sweats, I had scratches and bandages on my skin, my vagina was sore and had become a strange, dark color from all the prodding, my underwear was missing, and I felt too empty to continue to speak. That I was also afraid, that I was also devastated. That day we drove home and for hours my sister held me.

My boyfriend did not know what happened, but called that day and said, "I was really worried about you last night, you scared me, did you make it home okay?" I was horrified. That's when I learned I had called him that night in my blackout, left an incomprehensible voicemail, that we had also spoken on the phone, but I was slurring so heavily he was scared for me, that he repeatedly told me to go find my sister. Again, he asked me, "What happened last night? Did you make it home okay?" I said yes, and hung up to cry.

I was not ready to tell my boyfriend or parents that actually, I may have been raped behind a dumpster, but I don't know by who or when or how. If I told them, I would see the fear on their faces, and mine would multiply by tenfold, so instead I pretended the whole thing wasn't real.

I tried to push it out of my mind, but it was so heavy I didn't talk, I didn't eat, I didn't sleep, I didn't interact with anyone. After work, I would drive to a secluded place to scream. I didn't talk, I didn't eat, I didn't sleep, I didn't interact with anyone, and I became isolated from the ones I loved most. For one week after the incident, I didn't get any calls or updates about that night or what happened to me. The only symbol that proved that it hadn't just been a bad dream, was the sweatshirt from the hospital in my drawer.

One day, I was at work, scrolling through the news on my phone, and came across an article. In it, I read and learned for the first time about how I was found unconscious, with my hair disheveled, long necklace wrapped around my neck, bra pulled out of my dress, dress pulled off over my shoulders and pulled up above my waist, that I was butt naked all the way down to my boots, legs spread apart, and had been penetrated by a foreign object by someone I did not recognize. This was how I learned what happened to me, sitting at my desk reading the news at work. I learned what happened to me the same time everyone else in the world learned what happened to me. That's when the pine needles in my hair made sense, they didn't fall from a tree. He had taken off my underwear, his fingers had been inside of me. I don't even know this person. I still don't know this person. When I read about me like this, I said, this can't be me. This can't be me. I could not digest or accept any of this information. I could not imagine my family having to read about this online. I kept reading. In the next paragraph, I read something that I will never forgive; I read that according to him, I liked it. I liked it. Again, I do not have words for these feelings.

At the bottom of the article, after I learned about the graphic details of my own sexual assault, the article listed his swimming times. *She was found breathing, unresponsive with her underwear six inches away from her bare stomach curled in fetal position. By the way, he's really good at swimming.* Throw in my mile time if that's what we're doing. I'm good at cooking, put that in there, I think the end is where you list your extra-curriculars to cancel out all the sickening things that've happened.

The night the news came out I sat my parents down and told them that I had been assaulted, to not look at the news because it's upsetting, just know that I'm okay, I'm right here, and I'm okay. But halfway through telling them, my mom had to hold me because I could no longer stand up. I was not okay.

[…]

The night after it happened, he said he thought I liked it because I rubbed his back. A back rub. Never mentioned me voicing consent, never mentioned us speaking, a back rub.

[…]

I thought there's no way this is going to trial; there were witnesses, there was dirt in my body, he ran but was caught. He's going to settle, formally apologize, and we will both move on. Instead, I was told he hired a powerful attorney, expert witnesses, private investigators who were going to try and find details about my personal life to use against me, find loopholes in my story to invalidate me and my sister, in order to show that this sexual assault was in fact a misunderstanding. That he was going to go to any length to convince the world he had simply been confused.

I was not only told that I was assaulted, I was told that because I couldn't remember, I technically could not prove it was unwanted. And that distorted me, damaged me, almost broke me. It is the saddest type of confusion to be told I was assaulted and nearly raped, blatantly out in the open, but we don't know if it counts as assault yet. I had to fight for an entire year to make it clear that there was something wrong with this situation.

When I was told to be prepared in case we didn't win, I said, I can't prepare for that. He was guilty the minute I woke up. No one can talk me out of the hurt he caused me. Worst of all, I was warned, because he now knows you don't remember, he is going to get to write the script. He can say whatever he wants and no one can contest it. I had no power, I had no voice, I was defenseless. My memory loss would be used against me. My testimony was weak, was incomplete, and I was made to believe that perhaps, I am not enough to win this. That's so damaging. His attorney constantly reminded the jury, the only one we can believe is Brock, because she doesn't remember. That helplessness was traumatizing.

Instead of taking time to heal, I was taking time to recall the night in excruciating detail, in order to prepare for the attorney's questions that would be invasive, aggressive, and designed to steer me off course, to contradict myself, my sister, phrased in ways to manipulate my answers. Instead of his attorney saying, Did you notice any abrasions? He said, You didn't notice any abrasions, right? This was a game of strategy, as if I could be tricked out of my own worth. The sexual assault had been so clear, but instead, here I was at the trial, answering question like:

How old are you? How much do you weigh? What did you eat that day? Well what did you have for dinner? Who made dinner? Did you drink with dinner? No, not even water? When did you drink? How much did you drink? What container did you drink out of? Who gave you the drink? How much do you usually drink? Who dropped you off at this party? At what time? But where exactly? What were you wearing? Why were you going to this party? What'd you do when you got there? Are you sure you did that? But what time did you do that? What does this text mean? Who were you texting? When did you urinate? Where did you urinate? With whom did you urinate outside? Was your phone on silent when your sister called? Do you remember silencing it? Really because on page 53 I'd like to point out that you said it was set to ring. Did you drink in college? You said you were a party animal? How many times did you black out? Did you party at frats? Are you serious with your boyfriend? Are you sexually active with him? When did you start dating? Would you ever cheat? Do you have a history of cheating? What do you mean when you said you wanted to reward him? Do you remember what time you woke up? Were you wearing your cardigan? What color was your cardigan? Do you remember any more from that night? No? Okay, we'll let Brock fill it in.

I was pummeled with narrowed, pointed questions that dissected my personal life, love life, past life, family life, inane questions, accumulating trivial details to try and find an excuse for this guy who didn't even take the time to ask me for my name, who had me naked a handful of minutes after seeing me. After a physical assault, I was assaulted with questions designed to attack me, to say see, her facts don't line up, she's out of her mind, she's practically an alcoholic, she probably wanted to hook up, he's like an athlete right, they were both drunk, whatever, the hospital stuff she remembers is after the fact, why take it into account, Brock has a lot at stake so he's having a really hard time right now.

And then it came time for him to testify. This is where I became revictimized. I want to remind you, the night after it happened he said he never planned to take me back to his dorm. He said he didn't know why we were behind a dumpster. He got up to leave because he wasn't feeling well when he was suddenly chased and attacked. Then he learned I could not remember.

[…]

Your attorney has repeatedly pointed out, well we don't know exactly when she became unconscious. And you're right, maybe I was still fluttering my eyes and wasn't completely limp yet, fine. His guilt did not depend on him knowing the exact second that I became unconscious, that is never what this was about. I was slurring, too drunk to consent way before I was on the ground. I should have never been touched in the first place. Brock stated, "At no time did I see that she was not responding. If at any time I thought she was not responding, I would have stopped immediately." Here's the thing; if your plan was to stop only when I was literally unresponsive, then you still do not understand. You didn't even stop when I was unconscious anyway! Someone else stopped you. Two guys on bikes noticed I wasn't moving in the dark and had to tackle you. How did you not notice while on top of me?

You said, you would have stopped and gotten help. You say that, but I want you to explain how you would've helped me, step by step, walk me through this. I want to know, if those evil Swedes had not found me, how the night would have played out. I am asking you; Would you have pulled my underwear back on over my boots? Untangled the necklace wrapped around my neck? Closed my legs, covered me? Tucked my bra back into my dress? Would you have helped me pick the needles from my hair? Asked if the abrasions on my neck and bottom hurt? Would you then go find a friend and say, Will you help me get her somewhere warm and soft? I don't sleep when I think about the way it could have gone if the Swedes had never come. What would have happened to me? That's what you'll never have a good answer for, that's what you can't explain even after a year.

To sit under oath and inform all of us, that yes I wanted it, yes I permitted it, and that you are the true victim attacked by guys for reasons unknown to you is sick, is demented, is selfish, is stupid. It shows that you were willing to go to any length, to discredit me, invalidate me, and explain why it was okay to hurt me. You tried unyieldingly to save yourself, your reputation, at my expense.

[…]

You are guilty. Twelve jurors convicted you guilty of three felony counts beyond reasonable doubt, that's twelve votes per count, thirty-six yeses confirming guilt, that's one hundred percent, unanimous guilt. And I thought finally it is over, finally he will own up to what he did, truly apologize, we will both move on and get better. Then I read your statement.

If you are hoping that one of my organs will implode from anger and I will die, I'm almost there. You are very close. Assault is not an accident. This is not a story of another drunk college hookup with poor decision making. Somehow, you still don't get it. Somehow, you still sound confused.

I will now take this opportunity to read portions of the defendant's statement and respond to them.

You said, Being drunk I just couldn't make the best decisions and neither could she.

Alcohol is not an excuse. Is it a factor? Yes. But alcohol was not the one who stripped me, fingered me, had my head dragging against the ground, with me almost fully naked. Having too much to drink was an amateur mistake that I admit to, but it is not criminal. Everyone in this room has had a night where they have regretted drinking too much, or knows someone close to them who has had a night where they have regretted drinking too much. Regretting drinking is not the same as regretting sexual assault. We were both drunk, the difference is I did not take off your pants and underwear, touch you inappropriately, and run away. That's the difference.

You said, If I wanted to get to know her, I should have asked for her number, rather than asking her to go back to my room.

I'm not mad because you didn't ask for my number. Even if you did know me, I would not want be in this situation. My own boyfriend knows me, but if he asked to finger me behind a dumpster, I would slap him. No girl wants to be in this situation. Nobody. I don't care if you know their phone number or not. You said, I stupidly thought it was okay for me to do what everyone around me was doing, which was drinking. I was wrong. Again, you were not wrong for drinking. Everyone around you was not sexually assaulting me. You were wrong for doing what nobody else was doing, which was pushing your erect dick in your pants against my naked, defenseless body concealed in a dark area, where partygoers could no longer see or protect me, and own my sister could not find me. Sipping fireball is not your crime. Peeling off and discarding my underwear like a candy wrapper to insert your finger into my body, is where you went wrong. Why am I still explaining this.

You said, During the trial I didn't want to victimize her at all. That was just my attorney and his way of approaching the case.

Your attorney is not your scapegoat, he represents you. Did your attorney say some incredulously infuriating, degrading things? Absolutely. He said you had an erection, because it was cold. I have no words.

You said, you are in the process of establishing a program for high school and college students in which you speak about your experience to "speak out against the college campus drinking culture and the sexual promiscuity that goes along with that."

Speak out against campus drinking culture. That's what we're speaking out against? You think that's what I've spent the past year fighting for? Not awareness about campus sexual assault, or rape, or learning to recognize consent. Campus drinking culture. Down with Jack Daniels. Down with Skyy Vodka. If you want talk to high school kids about drinking go to an AA meeting. You realize, having a drinking problem is different than drinking and then forcefully trying to have sex with someone? Show men how to respect women, not how to drink less.

Drinking culture and the sexual promiscuity that goes along with that. Goes along with that, like a side effect, like fries on the side of your order. Where does promiscuity even come into play? I don't see headlines that read, *Brock Turner, Guilty of drinking too much and the sexual promiscuity that goes along with that.* Campus Sexaul Assault. There's your first powerpoint slide.

I have done enough explaining. You do not get to shrug your shoulders and be confused anymore. You do not get to pretend that there were no red flags. You do not get to not know why you ran. You have been convicted of violating me with malicious intent, and all you can admit to is consuming alcohol. Do not talk about the sad way your life was upturned because alcohol made you do bad things. Figure out how to take responsibility for your own conduct.

Lastly you said, I want to show people that one night of drinking can ruin a life.

Ruin a life, one life, yours, you forgot about mine. Let me rephrase for you, I want to show people that one night of drinking can ruin two lives. You and me. You are the cause, I am the effect. You have dragged me through this hell with you, dipped me back into that night again and again. You knocked down both our towers, I collapsed at the same time you did. Your damage was concrete; stripped of titles, degrees, enrollment. My damage was internal, unseen, I carry it with me. You took away my worth, my privacy, my energy, my time, my safety, my intimacy, my confidence, my own voice, until today.

See one thing we have in common is that we were both unable to get up in the morning. I am no stranger to suffering. You made me a victim. In newspapers my name was "unconscious intoxicated woman", ten syllables, and nothing more than that. For a while, I believed that that was all I was. I had to force myself to relearn my real name, my identity. To relearn that this is not all that I am. That I am not just a drunk victim at a frat party found behind a dumpster, while you are the All-American swimmer at a top university, innocent until proven guilty, with so much at stake. I am a human being who has been irreversibly hurt, who waited a year to figure out if I was worth something.

[…]

If you think I was spared, came out unscathed, that today I ride off into sunset, while you suffer the greatest blow, you are mistaken. Nobody wins. We have all been devastated, we have all been trying to find some meaning in all of this suffering.

You should have never done this to me. Secondly, you should have never made me fight so long to tell you, you should have never done this to me. But here we are. The damage is done, no one can undo it. And now we both have a choice. We can let this destroy us, I can remain angry and hurt and you can be in denial, or we can face it head on, I accept the pain, you accept the punishment, and we move on.

Your life is not over, you have decades of years ahead to rewrite your story. The world is huge, it is so much bigger than Palo Alto and Stanford, and you will make a space for yourself in it where you can be useful and happy. Right now your name is tainted, so I challenge you to make a new name for yourself, to do something so good for the world, it blows everyone away. You have a brain and a voice and a heart. Use them wisely. You possess immense love from your family. That alone can pull you out of anything. Mine has held me up through all of this. Yours will hold you and you will go on.

I believe, that one day, you will understand all of this better. I hope you will become a better more honest person who can properly use this story to prevent another story like this from ever happening again. I fully support your journey to healing, to rebuilding your life, because that is the only way you'll begin to help others.

Now to address the sentencing. When I read the probation officer's report, I was in disbelief, consumed by anger which eventually quieted down to profound sadness. My statements have been slimmed down to distortion and taken out of context.

[…]

I told the probation officer I do not want Brock to rot away in prison. I did not say he does not deserve to be behind bars. The probation officer's recommendation of a year or less in county jail is a soft time-out, a mockery of the seriousness of his assaults, and of the consequences of the pain I have been forced to endure. I also told the probation officer that what I truly wanted was for Brock to get it, to understand and admit to his wrongdoing.

Unfortunately, after reading the defendant's statement, I am severely disappointed and feel that he has failed to exhibit sincere remorse or responsibility for his conduct. I fully respected his right to a trial, but even after twelve jurors unanimously convicted him guilty of three felonies, all he has admitted to doing is ingesting alcohol. Someone who cannot take full accountability for his actions does not deserve a mitigating sentence. It is deeply offensive that he would try and dilute rape with a suggestion of promiscuity. By definition rape is the absence of promiscuity, rape is the absence of consent, and it perturbs me deeply that he can't even see that distinction.

The probation officer factored in that the defendant is youthful and has no prior convictions. In my opinion, he is old enough to know what he did was wrong. When you are eighteen in this country you can go to war. When you are nineteen, you are old enough to pay the consequences for attempting to rape someone. He is young, but he is old enough to know better.

As this is a first offense I can see where leniency would beckon. On the other hand, as a society, we cannot forgive everyone's first sexual assault or digital rape. It doesn't make sense. The seriousness of rape has to be communicated clearly, we should not create a culture that suggests we learn that rape is wrong through trial and error. The consequences of sexual assault needs to be severe enough that people feel enough fear to exercise good judgment even if they are drunk, severe enough to be preventative. The fact that Brock was a star athlete at a prestigious university should not be seen as an entitlement to leniency, but as an opportunity to send a strong cultural message that sexual assault is against the law regardless of social class.

The probation officer weighed the fact that he has surrendered a hard earned swimming scholarship. If I had been sexually assaulted by an un-athletic guy from a community college, what would his sentence be? If a first time offender from an underprivileged background was accused of three felonies and displayed no accountability for his actions other than drinking, what would his sentence be? How fast he swims does not lessen the impact of what happened to me.

The Probation Officer has stated that this case, when compared to other crimes of similar nature, may be considered less serious due to the defendant's level of intoxication. It felt serious. That's all I'm going to say.

[…]

And finally, to girls everywhere, I am with you. On nights when you feel alone, I am with you. When people doubt you or dismiss you, I am with you. I fought everyday for you. So never stop fighting, I believe you. Lighthouses don't go running all over an island looking for boats to save; they just stand there shining. Although I can't save every boat, I hope that by speaking today, you absorbed a small amount of light, a small knowing that you can't be silenced, a small satisfaction that justice was served, a small assurance that we are getting somewhere, and a big, big knowing that you are important, unquestionably, you are untouchable, you are beautiful, you are to be valued, respected, undeniably, every minute of every day, you are powerful and nobody can take that away from you. To girls everywhere, I am with you. Thank you.

4

Yes Means Yes

Jordan L. Metsky

Jordan L. Metsky is a DO candidate at the Western University of Health Sciences—College of Osteopathic Medicine of the Pacific-Northwest. She received her BA in bioethics from American University and researches the intersection of women's health and contemporary culture.

Using the passage of California Senate Bill 967 (SB-967) as a starting point for her discussion, Metsky argues that mutual consent is necessary not only for lowered prevalence of sexual assault but also for sexual pleasure. Known as the "Yes Means Yes" law, SB-967 states that mutual consent is required of all sexual activity; the absence of mutual consent means that a sexual crime has taken place. Metsky applauds this bill but takes its meaning one step further. Not only is mutual consent necessary for sexual violence prevention, but it also changes the meaning of sex itself. Mutual consent allows both partners to engage fully in pleasure and to cast off any fears or anxieties that often move sex from the domain of pleasure into the domain of oppression.

On September 28, 2014, California passed Senate Bill 967 (SB-967), requiring the governing boards of all institutions of higher education in California to adopt a uniform mutual and affirmative consent standard for those engaging in sexual activities.[1] Commonly known as the "Yes Means Yes" law, SB-967 explicitly disallows implied consent as an acceptable form of permission to engage in sexual activity. This bill marks the first implementation of uniform affirmative consent laws across college campuses on a statewide level.[2]

Here, I will argue that SB-967 is a crucial first step for America to open a needed and meaningful discourse on sexual intercourse. The passage of SB-967 highlights the lack of a meaningful discourse about sexual intercourse in the recent American consciousness. What is meant by a meaningful discourse on sex is one that will hold mutual consent as its main tenant, and will allow for a respectful, open, and shared discussion about sex between members of society. Data on sexual violence compiled by the National Institute of Justice indicate the stark effects of this dialogue's absence. One in four American college women is a survivor of rape or attempted rape,[3] with even higher rates for students who do not identify as heterosexual.[4]

The gravity of these sexual crimes is reflected by the fact that 80% of victims go on to suffer chronic health consequences.[5] Though more than 800 American colleges and universities have adopted a definition of sexual violence rooted in lack of consent[6], California is the first and only state to approve a uniform policy that defines mutual consent and uses it as a determination of the occurrence

1. De León K. California Senate Bill No. 967, Chapter 748. 2014.
2. Pérez-Pena R, Lovett I. California law on sexual consent pleases many but leaves some doubters. New York Times. September 30, 2014:A14.
3. Full report of the prevalence, incidence, and consequences of violence against women: Findings from the national violence against women survey. National Institute of Justice website. http://www.nij.gov/topics/ crime/violence-against-women/Pages/selectedresults .aspx#tjaden06. Published November 2000. Accessed October 14, 2014.
4. Campus sexual assault: Suggested policies and procedures. Academe [serial online]. Academic Search Elite, MA. July 2013; 99(4): 92-100. Accessed November 23, 2014.
5. Strategies for the treatment and prevention of sexual assault. American Medical Association website. www. ama-assn.org/ama1/pub/upload/mm/386/sexualassault.pdf. Published 1995. Accessed October 2, 2014.
6. The NCHERM group continues to advocate for affirmative consent policies in colleges and schools across the nation. PR Newswire website. http://www.prnewswire.com/news -releases/the-ncherm-group-continuesto-advocate-for-affirmative-consent-policies-in -colleges-and-schools-across-the-nation-278778841.html. Published October 10, 2014. Accessed November 23, 2014.

of sexual violence on college campuses.[2] So clandestine is the topic of sex, that even when a widespread problem has been occurring for decades, sex *still* fails to become an issue of well-known national import, and can instead become a site of oppression. One particular finding from The National Campaign to Prevent Teen and Unplanned Pregnancy's *With One Voice* study echoes the sentiment that Americans fail to adequately communicate about sexual issues: 87% of teens ages 12-19 agree that it would be easier to postpone sexual activity if they could "have more open, honest conversation about these topics with their parents."[7]

Americans have done a poor job of creating a social environment in which sex is respectfully but openly discussed. *With One Voice* illustrates how the immediate effects of a deficient cultural dialogue about sex manifest in teens and college-aged students. As a result, discussions of sex can become viewed as indecent[8], leaving no adequate space for open and shared discussions about sexual pleasure.

Required mutual consent is a first step toward creating an open dialogue about sex. SB-967 will require "an affirmative, unambiguous and conscious decision" by all involved actors to participate in a sexual encounter.[1] To satisfy the requirement of consent as defined by SB-967, those participating in sexual acts must discuss the acts with their partners. Because the ensuing behavior in a sexual situation must be expressed and agreed upon prior to initiation of the behavior, any participant in a sexual encounter governed by SB-967 will identify with his or her own role as an agent of sexuality through discussions of mutual consent. If these discussions are continuously carried out on a micro-level between sexual partners, it follows that mutual consent can be upheld as an agent of sexual discourse on a macro-level.

7. With one voice: America's adults and teens sound off about teen pregnancy. National campaign to prevent teen pregnancy website. http://thenationalcampaign. org/sites/default/files/resource-primary-download/ wov_2012.pdf. Published August 2012. Accessed October 20, 2014.
8. Wolf N. Why is it so difficult to talk about female sexual pleasure? Time. 2012. http:// ideas.time. com/2012/09/25/is-female-sexual-pleasure-devalued/. Accessed December 24, 2014.

Mutual consent represents a necessary starting point for positioning pleasure as a key element of sex, but further steps are necessary to fully realize a meaningful discourse on sexual intercourse. In *Madness and Civilization*, philosopher Michel Foucault writes, "People know what they do; frequently they know why they do what they do; but what they don't know is what what they do does."[9] In scenarios of mutual consent, actors must know what they are doing in order to express consent. By extension, it is reasonable to assume that these actors are thinking about why they are engaging in the sexual activity, including reasons of lust, love, or procreation. However, in order for sexual satisfaction to result, actors, as Foucault suggests, must think about what they are doing *does*. In other words, sexual actors must think about what constitutes the ontological end of sexual intercourse. This end—from making a partner climax to creating new life—may be different for each actor, and yet, no ends need be mutually exclusive from the creation of mutual pleasure. At worst, as indicated by austere sexual violence rates, sex without the mutually agreed upon end of pleasure remains a locus of oppression and control. Mutual consent, however, is not enough to realize pleasure as an end of sexual intercourse. In order to fully realize sex as pleasure, actors must talk *through* sex, as simply conferring on consent prior to engaging in sexual intercourse may not be enough to ensure consistent mutual consent.

Ideally, in a consensual setting, sexual actors engage in a dynamic of reciprocal expression. As a result, sex can result in consensual pleasure. In mandating the expression of mutual consent prior to sexual behavior, sex can be refocused as a locus of pleasure.

SB-967 represents a starting point in opening a discourse on sexual intercourse that is focused on pleasure and mutuality; however, it is not a flawless piece of legislation. Although it is not within the purview of this paper to address all of the weaknesses

9. Foucault M. Madness and Civilization: A history of insanity in the age of reason. New York, New York: Vintage Books; 1988.

of SB-967, the following section will discuss how SB-967 dubiously defines the notion of consent and how this definition can be problematic for the accused. The primary challenge in assessing the future impact of SB-967 lies in the bill's ambiguous definition of mutual consent, defining it only as "affirmative, conscious, and voluntary."[1] For example, while the bill does clearly state that intoxication precludes the provision of consent1, no specifications are given as to the degree of intoxication required to void one's ability to give consent, which would appropriately vary with one's physical makeup.

Without clearly describing what criteria must be met in order to satisfy mutual consent, the bill necessitates the interpretation of mutual consent by sexual actors. Considered in isolation, this ambiguity actually serves to perpetuate the opening of the dialogue on sexual intercourse. Rather than having a circumscribed set of qualifications that must be met to satisfy the threshold of mutual consent—which would refocus sex as a site of authority and oppression—actors must consciously define for themselves what standards constitute mutual consent and consider the conditions under which it might not be appropriate to engage in sexual intercourse. Considered within the context of the bill, however, the lack of clarity about what qualifies as mutual consent can pose a problem in considering how to proceed once an episode of sexual violence has been reported.

Because mutual consent is not clearly defined in the language of SB-967, and there are no prescribed parameters for its documentation, it then follows that there is due cause for an accusation of sexual violence if just one actor feels that the threshold for mutual consent was not met. Stated another way, individual dissent will disprove mutual consent. Given such a situation, there would appear to be no need to investigate an incident of sexual violence; so long as the reporter of the incident believes that consent was neither mutual nor affirmative, sexual violence must have occurred because the reporter said it did. If there is no official and required documentation of mutual consent, then each time a claim of sexual violence is made, the accused can theoretically be found guilty without further inquiry. The burden of proof to show that mutual affirmative consent was met then falls on the accused, and the process of substantiating claims of assault or violence are left wholly for each college or university to deal with independently.[10] As such, it is important to help validate the claim of the accuser while not forsaking due process for the accused.

The aims of an open discourse on sex include preventing sexual violence and helping to empower victims of sexual violence, but neither of these aims can be met if the rights of the accused are forsaken. As such, it is incumbent upon schools to adopt a policy that suggests how documentation of mutual consent may be collected so as to protect the rights of the accused and preserve the dignity of the accuser in situations of alleged sexual violence. The creation, deployment, and reformation of such policies on college campuses will serve as a preliminary step in opening discourse about sexual intercourse.

The implementation of SB-967 represents only the first step in a series of changes that must follow in order to make sure that mutual consent becomes central to discussions of safe and pleasurable sex. In order to incorporate the policy into a campus's culture, each college and university must create their own mutual consent policy that satisfies the parameters of the law. The White House Task Force to Prevent Students from Sexual Assault recommends that schools conduct campus climate surveys to determine students' attitudes about sexual violence,[11] and such surveys would help to create policies personalized for each individual school.

Although California is the first state to adopt a statewide policy on mutual affirmative consent on college campuses,[2] Antioch College in Ohio was one of the first colleges to support a policy

10. Gershman M. The Underside of "Affirmative Consent." The American Interest. http://www.the-american-interest.com/2014/10/19/the-underside-of-affirmative-consent/. Published 2014. Accessed November 21, 2014.
11. White House Task Force to Prevent Students from Sexual Assault. Not Alone: The First Report of the White House Task Force to Prevent Students from Sexual Assault. http://www.whitehouse.gov/sites/default/ files/docs/report_0.pdf. Updated April 2014. Accessed December 24, 2014.

of affirmative mutual consent, called the Sexual Offense Prevention Policy (SOPP) in 1991.[12] In discussing Antioch College's policy of mutual affirmative consent, concerned citizen Julia A. Reidhead writes in a letter to the editor of *The New Yorker* that a policy of mutual affirmative consent is "an opportunity for undergraduates to discover that wordplay and foreplay can be happily intertwined. The possibilities are wonderful-pedagogic, even-as is the idea that language is choice."[13]

A policy of mutual affirmative consent during sexual relations holds each sexual actor responsible for generating his or her own conception of consent and then communicating that consent during each step of sexual intercourse. By creating provisions to make sure that all sexual actors actively and continuously consent to engage in sex, the law empowers sexual actors by encouraging them to define and obtain mutual consent during each sex act, and provides the framework for sexual actors to begin to view the ontological end of sex as pleasure. Other states, including New Jersey and New Hampshire, have also introduced legislation aimed at creating statewide guidelines for affirmative consent on college campuses.[14]

High rates of sexual violence across college campuses indicate that a more open dialogue about sex is desperately needed nationwide. By targeting college campuses as sites of education and change, SB-967 has the potential to create widespread effects, including placing increased emphasis on mutual consent to sexual intercourse. As a law still in its infancy, it would be impractical to quantify the effects of SB-967, on reporting of sexual violence events on college campuses or on overall rates of sexual violence.

12. Antioch College. Student Handbook 2013-2014: Sexual offense prevention policy. http://www.antiochcollege.org/sites/default/files/pdf/student-handbook. pdf#page=42. Accessed November 25, 2014.

13. Guskin A. The antioch response: Sex, you just don't talk about it. In Francis L, ed. Date rape: feminism, philosophy, and the law. 1st ed. University Park, PA: Penn State University Press; 1996:158.

14. Schow A. Affirmative consent is spreading. Washington Examiner. http://www .washingtonexaminer.com/affirmative-consent-laws-spreading-across-theus/ article/2554754. Published October 14, 2014. Accessed November 23, 2014.

Further, such quantifications would greatly oversimplify the potential impact of the law. The essence of SB-967 lies in its ability to open a discourse on sexual intercourse between sexual actors that will bleed into a larger public discourse. When actors realize the ontological end of sex as pleasure and feel uninhibited to discuss sex, a reduction in sexual violence should logically follow.

The policy of mutual consent, as called for in SB-967, will require that sexual actors think through their behavior to understand consent as a vehicle for mutually desired and mutually pleasurable sex. As such, the bill represents a first step in working toward a meaningful American discourse on sexual intercourse. Ultimately, the bill's legacy will not be quantified by how many incidents of sexual violence it prevents, but instead, by how it reframes the way that people converse about and create shared experiences around sex. Continued discussions about sex and pleasure will contribute to the creation of a meaningful discourse on sexual intercourse and will transition sex from a site of oppression to a source of pleasure.

5

Even the Lowest Estimates of Campus Sexual Assault Are Far Too High

Elizabeth Armstrong and Jamie Budnick

Elizabeth Armstrong is a professor of sociology and organizational studies at the University of Michigan, where she specializes in sexuality, gender, and higher education. Her cowriter, Jamie Budnick, is a doctoral candidate in sociology at the University of Michigan.

There are many data about the prevalence of sexual assault on campus colleges. While major studies, including the White House task force, have claimed that 20 percent of undergraduate women will experience sexual assault in college, others have argued that the true incidence is much less. Armstrong and Budnick analyzed numerous public health studies to determine that actual incidence of sexual assault on campus. Using this data, they argue that between 14 and 26 percent of female undergraduates will experience sexual assault during their time in college. This number is not incredibly precise because of the number of women who do not report sexual assaults as well as the difference in opinion over what constitutes sexual assault and rape.

Recent scandals about sexual assaults on college campuses have provoked vehement debates about the scope of the problem. According to the White House task force formed to investigate the issue, 20 percent of undergraduate women—1 in 5—are sexually assaulted while in college. But some observers claim the problem

"Sexual Assault on Campus," by Elizabeth Armstrong, Council on Contemporary Families, April 20, 2015. Reprinted by permission.

has been blown way out of proportion. For example, Christina Hoff Sommers argued in a May 2014 article in *Time* magazine that this number is derived from biased samples and poorly-designed survey questions. Instead, she claims, only one-in-forty college women is a victim of rape or sexual assault.

Disagreement is not confined to political debate. In a 2011 report, the Bureau of Justice Statistics acknowledged that competing estimates of sexual violence have existed for two decades without ever being definitively resolved. In this brief we evaluate existing knowledge about the incidence and prevalence of sexual victimization of women attending American colleges and universities. We follow the Bureau of Justice Statistics definition of rape as a form of sexual assault that includes forced sexual intercourse, whether by physical or psychological coercion, involving penetration by the offender(s). We include in our definition of rape any act of sexual intercourse performed on an individual who is incapacitated as a result of being comatose, drugged, or asleep. To avoid ambiguity, we do *not* include sexual coercion or unwanted sexual contact such as grabbing or fondling—although the latter also meets the Bureau of Justice Statistics definition of sexual assault. Comparing multiple public health surveys—including nationally representative population surveys—we find it likely that between 7 and 10 percent of women experience forcible rape in college, and that somewhere between 14 and 26 percent experience sexual assault.

The National Crime Victimization Survey (NCVS)

The NCVS, conducted by the Bureau of Justice Statistics, is the nation's primary source of information about criminal victimization, collecting data annually from about 90,000 households, comprising 160,000 persons. It asks about a range of topics including robbery, simple and aggravated assault, theft, household burglary, and motor vehicle theft, as well as sexual victimization. It is the only such survey that has been fielded annually, using the same methods and questions, over a long period of time (since 1973). It is thus the only source for data on changes over time in the rates of sexual victimization in the U.S., and the most reliable source for comparing the rates of victimization of different groups in the population. Police reports offer another source of information about sexual victimization, but they are problematic because only a fraction of sexual victimizations are reported to the police.

Despite these advantages, questions have been raised about the reliability of NCVS estimates of sexual victimization. In 2011 the Bureau of Justice Statistics (BJS) asked the National Research Council, through its Committee on National Statistics, to convene an expert panel to investigate the possible underestimation of rape in the National Crime Victimization Survey (NCVS). National Academy of Sciences panels undergo rigorous peer review, and the entire committee must sign off on the final report, which gives their findings much weight in the scientific community. In this case, The Panel on Measuring Rape and Sexual Assault in Bureau of Justice Statistics Household Surveys (hereafter, "the Panel") identified methodological problems with the NCVS that may lead to significant undercounting of rape and sexual assault.

First, the panel found that the fact that the survey is explicitly about crime likely inhibits reporting of assaults. Studies have consistently shown that many women do not label as "rape" or define as criminal many sexual incidents that are unwanted and meet standards of forcible rape. Some respondents may also think that only events reported to the police should be reported on a government crime survey. Others may fear that reporting the assault as a "crime" will get the perpetrator in trouble—something they may not want to do if he is a relative or partner.

Second, the data collection mode of the NCVS does not ensure privacy. The interviewer is required to question everyone 12 and older at designated households, which means that all residents know what others are being asked. These oral interviews may be overhead. Even if not overheard, other members of the household may be suspicious if an interview takes a long time. Given the special stigmatization attached to sexual behavior, this lack of privacy may impede reporting. The Panel additionally found that the NCVS may have recorded a person's refusal to answer questions about sexual victimization as evidence that violence did not occur.

Third, there are serious problems with the questions about sexual victimization. The NCVS does not ask about incapacitated rape. It asks about "rape," attempted rape," and "other type of sexual attack"—but all these terms have ambiguous meanings. Unlike national public health surveys, which ask more behaviorally specific questions about sexual victimization, the NCVS terms failed to "describe behavior or convey the complexity of the intended concepts; a respondent might not realize that what she or he experienced did in fact fit the definition of attempted rape, and the questionnaire does not provide definitions."

An indication of how these features of the survey lead to under-reporting can be found in a systematic comparison of public health and criminal justice methodologies undertaken by Bonnie Fisher and colleagues as part of the National College Women Sexual Victimization Survey (NCWSV). The researchers worked with the Bureau of Justice Statistics to simultaneously conduct two studies using an experimental design. One set of respondents was asked questions about sexual victimization using a screening questionnaire asking 10 behavioral specific questions (e.g. "has anyone made you have sexual intercourse by using force or threatening to harm you or someone close to you?"). The other set of respondents was questioned using the NCVS protocol, which skipped people past any further questions about sexual victimization if they responded negatively to a question "have you been forced or coerced to engage in unwanted sexual activity?" The two studies were both in the field in 1996 and—aside from the question wording—employed exactly the same design. In both cases, participants were asked to report incidents that occurred within the approximately seven months "since school began in fall 1996."

The crime wording captured just 9.4 percent of the incidents of completed rape reported by respondents who were asked the behaviorally worded questions. No wonder the Panel found that even the most conservative of the public health surveys, the 1990 National Women's Study (NWS), produced an estimate of completed rape five times higher than that produced by the NCVS. The Panel judged the problems with the NCVS to be so fundamental that sexual victimization could not be accurately measured within the context of an omnibus crime survey. The Panel recommended that the Bureau of Justice Statistics develop a separate survey for measuring rape and sexual assault.

Declines in Rape and Sexual Assault Over Time

Although the National Crime Victimization Survey probably underreports rape and sexual assault, its methodology has been largely consistent over time. As a result, the NCVS may capture trends in violence even if it does not accurately estimate the absolute level at any particular time. NCVS data suggest that sexual victimization has declined over time. A Bureau of Justice Statistics report published in March 2013 and based on NVCS data, "Female Victims of Sexual Violence, 1994–2010" found that "From 1995 to 2005, the total rate of sexual violence committed against U.S. female residents age 12 or older declined 64%. … It then remained unchanged from 2005 to 2010." On the other hand, public health surveys do *not* show a decline in estimates of rapes over time—even when restricting analysis to questions about forcible rape.

Higher Victimization Rates of Young Women Not in College

It is often assumed that female college students are at increased risk compared to their peers of the same age who are not attending college. Yet a Bureau of Justice Statistics Report entitled "Rape And Sexual Assault Among College-Age Females, 1995-2013" published in December 2014 found that 18-to-24 year old females *not* enrolled in a post-secondary school were 1.2 times more likely to experience rape and sexual assault victimization than college students in the same age range. These estimates were drawn from the NCVS, which does not ask about rape while incapacitated as a result of drugs or alcohol. Since a substantial amount of rape and sexual assault on campus involves using alcohol as a means of rendering victims unable to resist, the above study may underestimate the risk to students. Still, as Jennifer Barber documents in her related policy brief, women who are not in college experience more intimate partner violence in dating and romantic relationships than college women. It is possible that alcohol-facilitated sexual assault may be more common among college women, while intimate partner violence may be more common among non-college women.

Surveys of College Women: Prevalence of Sexual Assault

The NCVS is not the only source of data on the incidence and prevalence of rape and sexual assault. We focus here on the results of five different surveys of college women's sexual victimization conducted between 1984 and 2014.

We compared responses to the question about forced sexual intercourse across the five surveys, throwing out the highest estimate (which included rapes since age 14, and which was conducted in 1984) and the lowest estimate (which included only women attending MIT and did not isolate seniors). The College Sexual Assault (CSA) and Online College Social Life (OCSLS) surveys asked college seniors about the entirety of their time in college, producing estimates of 7 percent and 10 percent, respectively. The third study, the National College Women Sexual Victimization (NCWSV), asked only about incidents that occurred in the last 7 months. Multiplying the 1.7 percent incidence found in that survey by 5 (to cover 35 months on campus) offers a rough estimate of the risk over the course of college. This produced an estimated prevalence rate of 8.5. Taken together, these studies suggest that between 7 and 10 percent of undergraduate women experience forcible rape in college.

To calculate the prevalence of sexual assault in college, we combined responses to the question about forced sex with questions about incapacitated and attempted rape. The Online College Social Life (OCSLS) survey asked respondents these questions: "Since you started college, has someone tried to physically force you to have sexual intercourse, but you got out of the situation without having intercourse?" and "Since you started college, has someone had sexual intercourse with you that you did not want when you were drunk, passed out, asleep, drugged, or otherwise incapacitated?" Focusing on the three surveys above, we found affirmative responses ranging from 14 to 26 percent. That the estimates range from about 1 in 7 to 1 in 4 is not satisfying—but even the lowest one is far higher than the 1 in 40 number that Hoff Sommers cited, and they do *not* include cases of unwanted touching, grabbing, or fondling or psychological coercion (e.g. situations where individuals consent to sex after begging or pleading).

These surveys suggest that the 1 in 5 statistic so frequently quoted is reasonable, even though inexact. The two most comparable recent surveys—the CSA and OCSLS—converge on a figure of 25 to 26 percent of college women experiencing sexual assault in college—as Jessie Ford and Paula England note in a recent discussion of the finding of the Online College Social Life Survey.

The results of these surveys are certainly not definitive. The Campus Sexual Assault (CSA) survey studied only two universities and all the surveys had small sample sizes. Only two of the studies employed a national sampling frame. The problem is less with the flaws of particular studies, and more with the lack of a sustained national investment in collecting high quality data on the issue. The federal government only initiated a large-scale, annual, nationally representative public health survey of sexual victimization in 2010—the National Intimate Partner and Sexual Violence Survey (NISVS). This survey found that 12.3 percent of women of all ages reported having experienced forced intercourse. Because young women are more at risk of sexual victimization, this is compatible with the estimate that 7 to 10 percent of women experience forcible rape in college.

We were also able to compare the above surveys with highly regarded demographic surveys. These surveys asked only a few questions about sexual victimization and did not focus on college women, but nonetheless served as a useful check on the results of the surveys discussed above. For example, we looked at the National Survey of Family Growth (NSFG), which is conducted by the Centers for Disease Control. Based on a large (n=@19,000) nationally representative sample, it is the most widely used source of information about patterns of pregnancy, contraception, and fertility in the U.S. This survey found that just under 20 percent of 20–24 year old women surveyed in 2002 reported having ever experienced forced intercourse.

Conclusion

There are several reasons we do not have better data. Attitudes about what forms of nonconsensual sex are unacceptable have been in flux throughout the period under discussion in this report. In historical terms, changes in laws and attitudes about nonconsensual sex have been rapid: rape within marriage was not criminalized in all 50 U.S. states until 1993. Even now, some people view nonconsensual grabbing and fondling of young women as normal and acceptable, particularly when young women are socializing with same-age peers. What constitutes consent and what forms of unwanted sexual activity constitute assault continue to be contested.

In addition, gender-based violence has not been a central concern of U.S. family demographers or the National Institutes of Health, despite the fact that gender-based violence may be related to outcomes such as early and unintended pregnancy, inconsistent contraceptive use, engagement in risky health behaviors, and educational attainment.

Despite the limits of the existing data, we can all agree that even the lowest estimates represent substantial numbers of women who experience sexual assault or rape, and surely we can also agree that better data is needed to develop appropriate responses to sexual violence on campus and beyond, as well as to determine what preventative measures are most likely to work. We should encourage the Bureau of Justice Statistics to implement the recommendations of the Panel on Measuring Rape and Sexual Assault in Bureau of Justice Statistics Household Surveys. For now, though, we believe it is reasonable—even conservative—to work on the assumption that without stronger preventive action, somewhere between 14 and 26 percent of female undergraduates will experience sexual assault during their time in college.

References

Abbey, A. (2002). Alcohol-related Sexual Assault: A Common Problem among College Students. *Journal of Studies on Alcohol and Drugs*, (14), 118. Retrieved from http://collegedrinkingprevention.gov/media/Journal/118-Abbey.pdf

Barber, J.S., Kusunoki, Y., & Budnick, J. (2015). "Women who are not enrolled in four-year universities and colleges have higher risk of sexual assault."

Black, M. C., Basile, K. C., Breiding, M. J., Smith, S. G., Walters, M. L., Merrick, M. T., & Stevens, M. R. (2011). *National Intimate Partner and Sexual Violence Survey.* Atlanta, GA: CDC. Centers for Disease Control and Prevention. Retrieved from http://www.cdc.gov/ViolencePrevention/pdf/NISVS_Report2010-a.pdf

Burcau of Justice Statistics. (1973 2013). *Data Collection: National Crime Victimization Survey (NCVS).*Retrieved from http://www.bjs.gov/index.cfm?ty=dcdetail&iid=245

Bureau of Justice Statistics. (2011). *BJS Activities on Measuring Rape and Sexual Assault.* Retrieved from http://www.bjs.gov/content/pub/pdf/bjs_amrsa_poster.pdf

Bureau of Justice Statistics. (2013) *Female Victims of Sexual Violence, 1994-2010.* Retrieved from http://www.bjs.gov/content/pub/pdf/fvsv9410.pdf

Bureau of Justice Statistics. (2014). *Rape And Sexual Assault Among College-Age Females, 1995-2013.* (NCJ 248471). Retrieved from http://www.bjs.gov/content/pub/pdf/rsavcaf9513.pdf

Chandra, A., Martinez, G. M., Mosher, W. D., Abma, J. C., & Jones, J. (2005). "Fertility, Family Planning, and Reproductive Health of US Women: Data from the 2002 National Survey of Family Growth. *Vital and Health Statistics. Series 23, Data from the National Survey of Family Growth*, (25), 1-160. Retrieved from http://www.cdc.gov/nchs/data/series/sr_23/sr23_025.pdf

Fisher, B. S. (2009). "The Effects of Survey Question Wording on Rape Estimates: Evidence from a Quasi-experimental Design." *Violence Against Women*, 15, 133- 147. Retrieved fromhttp://vaw .sagepub.com/content/15/2/133.short. See also https://www.ncjrs .gov/pdffiles1/nij/199705.pdf

Fisher, B., Cullen, F. & Turner, M. (2000). *The Sexual Victimization of College Women*. (NCJ #182369.) Washington, DC: U.S. Department of Justice, National Institute of Justice. Retrieved from https://www.ncjrs.gov/pdffiles1/nij/182369.pdf

Fisher, B., Daigle, L., Cullen, F., & Turner, M. (2003). "Acknowledging Sexual Victimization as Rape: Results from a National-Level Study." *Justice Quarterly* 20(3), 535-574. Retrieved from http:// www.tandfonline.com/doi/abs/10.1080/07418820300095611# .VRh1Vjt4odU

Forbes, J., and England, P. (2015). "What Percent of College Women are Sexually Assaulted in College?"*Contexts* online blog, published by the American Sociological Association. Retrieved from http://contexts.org/blog/what-percent-of-college-women -are-sexually-assaulted-in-college/

Kilpatrick, D.G., Edmunds, C., & Seymour, A. (1992). *Rape in America: A Report to the Nation.* Charleston, SC: National Victim Center & the Crime Victims Research and Treatment Center, Medical University of South Carolina. Retrieved from https:// www.victimsofcrime.org/docs/Reports%20and%20Studies/rape -in-america.pdf?sfvrsn=0

Koss, M. P., Gidycz, C. A., & Wisniewski, N. (1987). "The Scope of Rape: Incidence and Prevalence of Sexual Aggression and Victimization in a National Sample of Higher Education Students." *Journal of Consulting and Clinical Psychology*, 55, 162-170. Retrieved from http://www.ncbi.nlm.nih.gov/ pubmed/3494755

Krebs, C.P., Lindquist, C.H., Warner, T.D., Fisher, B.S., & Martin, S.L. (2007). *The Campus Sexual Assault (CSA) Study.*

Washington, DC: National Institute of Justice, U.S. Department of Justice. Retrieved from https://www.ncjrs.gov/pdffiles1/nij/ grants/221153.pdf

Kruttschnitt, C., Kalsbeek, W. D., & House, C. C. (Eds.). (2014). *Estimating the Incidence of Rape and Sexual Assault.* National Academies Press. Retrieved from http://www.nap.edu/ catalog/18605/estimating-the-incidence-of-rape-and-sexual -assault. For a report brief http://sites.nationalacademies.org/cs/ groups/dbassesite/documents/webpage/dbasse_085943.pdf

Massachusetts Institute of Technology. (2014). *Survey Results: 2014 Community Attitudes on Sexual Assault.*Retrieved from http:// web.mit.edu/surveys/health/

Miller, Jody. (2008). *Getting Played: African American Girls, Urban Inequality, and Gendered Violence.* New York: New York University Press.

White House. (2014). *Not Alone: The First Report of the White House Task Force to Protect Students from Sexual Assault.* Washington, DC. Retrieved from http://www.whitehouse.gov/sites/default/ files/docs/report_0.pdf

6

The Accused Are Denied Due Process in Campus Sexual Assaults

Cathy Young

Cathy Young is a journalist who often writes about rape and feminism, oftentimes critiquing modern feminist thought and arguing that sexual abuse is over-reported. She is the author of two books and is a regular columnist for Newsday *and* Time.

In this article, Cathy Young, who is known for arguing that rape victims are not telling the truth, attempts to poke holes in Emma Sulkowicz's account of sexual assault. She shines the light on Sulkowicz's alleged rapist, Paul Nungesser, who states that he has been the victim of a campaign of lies against him. Young uses Sulkowicz's behavior toward Nungesser as evidence against her and meditates on the way in which due process can be suspended during such well known cases of alleged sexual assault. Young also takes the media to task for reporting on such cases before they are tried in a court of law.

At least for now, Columbia's mattress saga is over. Emma Sulkowicz, the student who spent her final year on campus toting a mattress to protest the school's failure to punish her alleged rapist, graduated at the end of May; so did Paul Nungesser, the accused man who says he's the real victim.

There was more drama at graduation: Sulkowicz toted her mattress onstage in defiance of school regulations and later accused Columbia president Lee Bollinger of snubbing her. In related news,

"Did 'Mattress Girl' Tell the Truth? Not Very Likely," by Cathy Young, mindingthecampus. org, June 4, 2015. Reprinted by permission.

posters branding Sulkowicz a liar cropped up near the campus; Nungesser was reported cleared on the last sexual assault complaint against him, this one from a male student; and, the next day, one of his two anonymous female accusers told her story on the feminist blog Jezebel.

An attempt at summing up this messy saga and its lessons comes from Emily Bazelon via Sunday's *New York Times Magazine*. Bazelon admits that *l'affaire Sulkowicz* drama highlights major problems with the current system of Title IX-based campus "justice"—including "utter lack of transparency," which is not a bug but a feature of the system: federal law stringently protects the privacy of students involved in disciplinary cases. As a result, in an alleged rape case that has attracted international attention and scrutiny, we are mostly left with he said/she said accounts not only of what happened between Nungesser and his accusers, but of how the complaints were handled by the university. The records exist, including transcripts and video recordings of the hearings; but they are off-limits and likely to remain so.

Dispensing with Due Process

Bazelon believes this fiasco is a result of the current system's growing pains—of "a transitional period in the evolution of how universities handle sexual assault." But it's hard to see what reforms would fix the problem. Even if school staff are better trained to investigate sexual misconduct reports—assuming that "better training" actually means more effective fact-finding, not more faithful adherence to believe-the-survivor dogma—this would not address the underlying issue: that activists like Sulkowicz want to dispense with any semblance of due process and refuse to respect any result other than culpability and punishment.

(Incidentally, while Bazelon correctly notes that "rape is extremely difficult to prosecute both effectively and fairly," the kind of violent attack that Sulkowicz alleges—an excruciatingly painful anal rape during which she was hit in the face, choked within an inch of her life, and pinned by the arms—would be quite easy to prove, at least if promptly reported to the police. The physical evidence would have been overwhelming.)

One lesson of this case Bazelon doesn't mention is that if universities are going to have rules for the disposition of Title IX cases, they need, at least, to enforce those rules in a fair and meaningful way. As Nungesser's lawsuit against Columbia points out, all the parties in sexual misconduct cases are urged to do what they can protect the confidentiality of the process and the privacy of all those involved. Sulkowicz has repeatedly violated that rule with impunity; the male accuser, known as "Adam," talked to Jezebel about his complaint while it was still under investigation, apparently with no consequences.

On Fulsome Display

Columbia's craven acquiescence to Sulkowicz's activism was on fulsome display in the graduation dust-up. A university email sent the previous day had reminded students not to bring large objects into the ceremonial area. When Sulkowicz arrived toting her mattress, she was apparently asked to stow it away for the ceremony; she refused, and she and her helpers were finally allowed onstage anyway. The university's official statement, emailed to me by director of communications Victoria Benitez, noted, "We were not going to physically block entry to graduates who are ultimately responsible for their own choices." In other words, compliance with the rules is a personal choice.

Another lesson is that the media need to exercise due diligence and skepticism when it comes to "survivor" narratives: not to treat accusers as presumptive liars, of course, but to ask questions and do the fact-checking. (In other words, "trust but verify.") That is something journalists egregiously failed to do for months, when Sulkowicz's narrative went unchallenged amidst massive publicity. The mainstream coverage today is much more balanced; Bazelon clearly presents this as a story with two sides and mentions some of the exculpatory evidence, including Sulkowicz's chatty Facebook messages to Nungesser after the alleged rape.

Yet even now, failure to verify remains a problem. No one, as far as I can tell, has followed up on Sulkowicz's claim (made in the annotations to her Facebook messages for Jezebel last February but never mentioned before or since) that the day after she was allegedly raped by Nungesser, she talked about it to a female friend "who explain[ed] it was rape." If such a corroborating witness exists, why did she not testify at the hearing or come forward to support Sulkowicz? Can Sulkowicz give this friend's name to journalists, at least on the condition that she won't be publicly identified?

To state the obvious, the truth in this story is ultimately unknowable. But here's what we do know.

Kept up A Friendly Act

Sulkowicz's account of her rape strains credulity to the extreme. Sulkowicz accuses Nungesser of an extremely brutal assault that should have left her visibly injured (with bruises not only on her face but on her neck and arms, unlikely to be covered by clothing in August and early September in New York) and in need of medical attention. Yet no one saw anything amiss after this attack, and both Nungesser and Sulkowicz went on to chat and banter on Facebook as if nothing happened. Sulkowicz's claim that she kept up a friendly act hoping to confront him about the rape seems extremely dubious, given the near-psychotic violence she alleges and the lack of any sign of unease or tension in their online conversations. (When I reread these archives recently, I checked the timestamps to see if there were any awkward pauses; there weren't, not even when Nungesser asks Sulkowicz to bring more girls to his party and she replies, "I'll be dere w da females soon.")

Is Sulkowicz a "false accuser"? We don't know that. It's possible that something ambiguous happened between her and Nungesser that night—something that she later came to see as coercive and embellished with violent details. But I would say the odds of her account being factually true are very low.

Sulkowicz has demonstrable credibility problems. A few examples:

- As Nungesser's lawsuit notes, at one point in spring 2014 Sulkowicz wrote that she lived in daily terror of encountering her rapist on campus—while another statement she made around the same time shows that she knew he was spending a semester in Europe. Prior to her claim that she spoke to a friend the morning after the alleged rape, Sulkowicz had sometimes asserted that she didn't tell anyone for several months, sometimes that she told a few friends. Last fall, Sulkowicz told the *Times'* Ariel Kaminer that after filing a police report, she had elected not to pursue criminal charges because the process would be "lengthy" and "too draining." Now, she tells Bazelon that she stopped talking to investigators because "the police were visiting her apartment unexpectedly."

- The multiple charges in this instance do not make for a stronger case because they are demonstrably linked to each other; what's more, there is evidence backing Nungesser's claim that he was targeted for a vendetta based on the belief that he had raped Sulkowicz.

- One of the other two female accusers, "Natalie"—Nungesser's freshman-year girlfriend—filed a complaint after talking to Sulkowicz and (in Sulkowicz's words) delving into their "shared trauma." Her complaint was dismissed for lack of evidence after she stopped cooperating with investigators. Nungesser's lawsuit says she claimed she felt obligated to have sex with him; Natalie herself told Bwog, the Columbia campus magazine, that he would often forcefully pin her arms back during sex and that she often cried when they were in bed. (She struggled with major depression during their relationship.)

Rape or Drunken Pass?

- "Josie," the accuser who authored the piece for Jezebel, admits that she filed her complaint with the encouragement of a "friend" who told her that Nungesser had been accused of raping another woman. As I have previously reported, that friend—to whom I have referred by the pseudonym "Leila"—was an officer in the Alpha Delta Phi coed fraternity to which Nungesser, Sulkowicz, and Josie all belonged. At the time, Leila was trying to get Nungesser ejected from the ADP residence because of Sulkowicz's charges. (Josie also lived at the house; Sulkowicz did not.)Josie's charge is the only one on which Nungesser was initially found culpable; that finding was later reversed on appeal, and a second hearing exonerated Nungesser after Josie declined to participate.Josie has given somewhat contradictory accounts of her decision to withdraw from the process. Among other things, she has repeatedly stressed that she had graduated from Columbia by then, without mentioning that the first hearing also took place months after her graduation in May 2013. (According to the timeline compiled by Nungesser's parents, the original hearing was held September 26; the appeal was granted on October 28, and the second hearing was on December 13.) Even if Josie's story is true, her complaint hardly corroborates Sulkowicz's accusation. Sulkowicz is alleging a brutal rape; Josie is alleging a boorish drunken pass at a booze-soaked frat party. She says that Nungesser followed her upstairs after offering to help restock the bar, then tried to kiss her and pulled her toward him despite her protestations, until she pushed him off and left. Such behavior may meet the definition of sexual assault on the modern campus, but it is hardly the mark of a violent sexual predator. Josie herself says she did not think of it as "sexual assault" until she heard about the alleged attack on Sulkowicz.

- The last and fourth charge from "Adam" has been all but definitively exposed as a fabrication, as I wrote on Reason .com last month after reviewing a leaked internal report by Columbia Title IX investigators. The report describes Adam as a highly "unreliable" complainant, partly because social media records contradicted his version of his interactions with Nungesser and backed Nungesser's. Adam also made bizarrely paranoid claims that Nungesser "retaliated" for his complaint—*before* the complaint was filed—by sitting too close to him and his friends in class and complimenting a point he had made in a class discussion. The document also reveals that Adam first made his allegations to Leila while she was collecting accusations of sexual misconduct against Nungesser in the wake of Sulkowicz's charge. Without explicitly confirming the existence of a vendetta, it notes that "at the time of the Complainant's initial disclosure, at least several of his close friends ... were [seeking] to evict the Respondent from the fraternity house." Adam was a close friend of Natalie's; Nungesser's lawsuit also alleges he is a close friend of Sulkowicz's.

Uncritical Reporters

While this is purely speculative, it is also interesting to note that the accusations against Nungesser first emerged in the immediate aftermath of the Steubenville, Ohio rape trial in February-March 2013, when the moral panic about "rape culture" reached fever pitch in the media and "sexual awareness" events proliferated on college campuses. Is it possible that this atmosphere of hypercharged rhetoric about the ubiquity of sexual violence and its tacit toleration by American society encouraged at least some of the complainants to reinterpret their own experiences as assaultive?

With Nungesser's lawsuit still pending, the story is certain to be back in the news. Perhaps, by the time it reaches its next round in the news cycle, the journalists who cover this case will learn some of its lessons and ask the hard questions.

In the meantime, there is certainly enough evidence to grant Nungesser the benefit of reasonable doubt not only in legal disciplinary proceedings, but in the court of public opinion. That is something he has been denied by Sulkowicz's campaign and its mostly uncritical media reception.

7

The Myth of a Rape Epidemic on Campus

Sean Collins

Sean Collins is a journalist for the online magazine Spiked, *where he writes about American current affairs. His writing has appeared in* American Conservative, *the* New York Post, *the* New York Times, *and the* Huffington Post, *among other outlets.*

In a now well-known case, Rolling Stone *magazine reported on a story about a woman who claimed to have been gang-raped at a University of Virginia fraternity. However, following publication, the story was retracted when evidence came to light that did not support the woman's statements. Sean Collins argues that such false media accounts feed into the myth of a rape epidemic on American campuses. In fact, Collins states, "rape culture" as such does not exist, and the occurrence of sexual assault on campus is much less prevalent than we would think.*

For years now, academics and activists, backed by university administrators and government officials, have promoted the idea that there is a rape epidemic on US campuses, enabled by a "rape culture" that pervades social life. This notion has created a frenzied and highly emotional atmosphere in colleges, with accusations flying and campus tribunals handing down sentences for what are essentially criminal acts. The stunning news that *Rolling Stone* now disowns its story that claimed a female student was gang-raped at a University of Virginia (UVA) fraternity shows

"*Rolling Stone* and the Myth of a Rape Epidemic," by Sean Collins, *Spiked*, December 8, 2014. Reprinted by permission.

that the drive to root out "rape culture" is spinning out of control. We're living through a full-blown panic, akin to the daycare sexual abuse scandals of the 1980s and early 1990s, with bad consequences for both women and men.

The *Rolling Stone* article, written by Sabrina Rubin Erdely, described in graphic terms how a young woman, "Jackie," was lured by her date to a room in a fraternity, where she was allegedly raped by seven men, as part of a premeditated initiation ceremony. The terrible details included: smashing Jackie through a plate-glass table, cutting her badly; the men laughing in response to her cries, and saying things like "grab its motherfucking leg"; the men calling each other names like Armpit and Blanket. Appearing after a three-hour ordeal, three friends discourage Jackie from reporting this to the police or the university, or from going to a hospital, because they fear they will be banned from future parties at this fraternity.

After some began to raise questions, an investigation by the *Washington Post* unearthed details that contradicted the story: the fraternity didn't hold a party on the date cited by Jackie; the man named as the alleged attacker belonged to a different fraternity, and he says he never met Jackie; no member of the fraternity worked as a lifeguard, as Jackie claimed her attacker did; the fraternity doesn't have a pledging or initiation process in Autumn, when the alleged attack was said to have occurred; a male friend of Jackie says she was not found in a bloody dress that night, nor did he or others try to dissuade her from reporting an assault. In the face of such revelations, *Rolling Stone* backtracked and apologised to its readers.

The unravelling of the *Rolling Stone* article is not an isolated event, nor simply the case of one journalist's lapse in ethics. The *New York Times* has highlighted cases at colleges such as Columbia and Hobart and William Smith, among others, in a similar way to *Rolling Stone*'s latest, focusing on the accuser's allegations at the expense of the full picture (an enterprising journalist might revisit these stories, too). But more importantly, the UVA story is the product of a fevered atmosphere whipped up by "rape culture" campaigners, an atmosphere where advocacy and emotion override fact.

Central to the myth of a rape epidemic is a statistic: that one in five women are sexually assaulted on US campuses over four years. The survey from which this statistic derives has been thoroughly debunked by Christina Hoff Sommers and others, who note, in particular, that the survey was based on a small sample (two schools) and a definition of assault so broad as to include uninvited touching and kissing, which even most respondents did not think rose to the level of an attack. In fact, according to more reliable Department of Justice data, sexual assault has *fallen* by more than 50 per cent in recent years, to a rate of 1.1 per 1,000 women, with similar rates on and off campus.

This of course directly contradicts claims made by promoters of a supposed rape epidemic. Indeed, the one-in-five statistic should be dismissed outright as utterly fantastic. If accepted, it would mean that violent crimes like rape are many times more likely to be found among the children of the elite on bucolic campuses than among those in the most dangerous inner cities. Are we really to believe that women on Yale's campus, based in New Haven, are raped at a rate of five per cent a year (according to campaigners, taking the one-in-five and dividing by four years), while in downtown New Haven the rate is 0.09 per cent (according to the FBI)? After the *Rolling Stone* fiasco, many are wondering how so many were willing to believe wild stories about gang rape. A better, less-asked question is: why do so many readily accept a bogus one-in-five statistic?

The White House has pushed the rape-epidemic notion, launching a campaign earlier this year called "It's on us," which seeks to combat sexual assault on campus. Before that, the Obama administration pressured colleges to introduce a parallel system of adjudication that bypasses the legal system. In 2011, the Department of Education warned that failure to act on sexual violence, including setting up rape tribunals, could be in violation of Title IX, an anti-discrimination law, and could be punished with a withdrawal of federal funding (even the richest private colleges receive such funding). These tribunals are effectively kangaroo courts, aimed to increase the likelihood of conviction: the standard is "preponderance of evidence" (50.1 per cent likelihood) rather than "beyond a reasonable doubt," and defendants are denied due-process rights, such as the right to review evidence, be represented by legal counsel and cross-examine witnesses. Those found guilty are expelled.

This government move has increased the number of accusations, as well as expulsions. But it has also led to a rise in lawsuits by expelled students claiming miscarriages of justice. Combined with government-demanded "training" on sexual assault, this topic has become an obsession on campus.

The controversy over the *Rolling Stone* article can only be understood if placed in the context of this febrile climate on America's campuses today. The search for a "rape culture" infused this story, from its rise to its fall. Consider:

- Erdely was on a mission to write about campus rape culture, and that campaigning style of journalism is what ultimately led her to put agenda before fact. She was pointed to Jackie by Emily Renda, a UVA advocate for those who claim to be victims of sexual assault, and took Jackie at her word, without attempting to speak to the accused or carry out further investigation.

- But it was not just Erdely. *Rolling Stone* withheld judgment and didn't feel the need to undertake basic fact-checking. Like Erdely, it initially found Jackie "credible," and that was enough.

- Upon publication, the article was greeted as a major contribution to the discussion. Feminists hailed it as proof of how blatant sexual attacks are, and how insensitive universities are in response. Many others suspended critical faculties and, no matter how outlandish and unbelievable the details, fell for the story—mainly because media discussion has largely accepted the message from the "rape culture" advocates about how fraternities and male students are hotbeds of sexual violence .

- When a few brave folk began to raise questions about Erdely's story, they were denounced as "rape apologists," "truthers" and "idiots." Such closeminded and defensive responses should have set off alarm bells widely, but didn't.

The exposure of Erdely and *Rolling Stone*'s handiwork as a fraud should be a challenge to the rape-culture myth. But instead, proponents of the myth doubled down on it, and said that the debunking of the story should lead us to *increase* efforts to combat the supposed scourge of rape on campus. *Mother Jones* quickly warned: "Don't let the *Rolling Stone* controversy distract you from the rape epidemic."

Expressing very little if any concern for the reputations of the men and fraternities at UVA accused by Jackie, many expressed worry that the storm over *Rolling Stone*'s piece would be most damaging to future victims, who, they said, may not be "believed." Zerlina Maxwell went as far as to say: "We should believe, as a matter of default, what an accuser says." This, of course, is exactly what Erdely did with Jackie, and exactly what led to the *Rolling Stone* debacle in the first place. We don't know for sure how many false allegations are made—and maybe they are a small minority, as campaigners claim—but clearly they do exist. And unfortunately today's defining down what is meant by assault, and the validation of victimhood, only encourages false accusations.

The call to "believe" victims is reminiscent of Salem. It is not a question of naively "believing" or "disbelieving" those who claim to be victims of sexual assault; it is a matter of ascertaining fact. For the sake of justice, we need to be sceptical of those who make allegations, and provide the accused with due process. In contrast, supporters of the rape-culture myth interpret any search for truth as a betrayal of the accuser, which is a truly medieval approach.

Ironically, those who promote the idea that rape is everywhere do not take rape seriously enough. They ignore that an accusation of rape is a very serious charge, which requires fact (indeed, questioning of the accuser shows that it is being taken seriously). They seek to have the alleged perpetrators kicked off campus, but, if they really are guilty of such a heinous crime, they should be sent away to prison and thus prevented from harming others. And they overlook how expulsion from college for reasons of rape can ruin someone's reputation and career.

Feminist activists are not the only ones who are doubling down in the aftermath of the *Rolling Stone* mess: so, too, are the administrators. In response to the article's initial publication, UVA president Teresa Sullivan referred to sexual violence on campus as an "evil," and banned activities by *all* fraternities (talk about collective guilt). And now that the story has collapsed... UVA is still continuing on the same path of bureaucratic review, and there has been no sign of lifting the outrageous ban on fraternities.

As these responses show, the "rape epidemic" has become an article of faith. Even the revelation of flimsy or no evidence in particular cases is not enough to shake this dogma. The entire claim of a rape culture needs to be exposed as being just as fictitious as the UVA gang-rape story.

8

Statistics About Rape and Sexual Assault on Campus Are Questionable

Jake New

Jake New is a reporter who covers student life and athletics for Inside Higher Ed. *His work has appeared in many outlets, and he is the recipient of the David W. Miller Award for Young Journalists.*

In this article, Jake New questions the often-heard statistic that one in five women on college campuses will experience sexual assault. New interviews advocates who are frustrated with the media attention this statistic has received, particularly because their research has shown them that the prevalence of sexual assault on campus is even higher. The difficulty of agreeing on statistics about rape and sexual assault, New argues, is because of the different definitions of what can be vague terms. For example, some studies include kissing and groping in their definition of rape, while others only count sexual penetration.

If there's a conversation taking place about the prevalence of campus sexual assault in the United States, the phrase "one in five" is usually within earshot.

"It is estimated that one in five women on college campuses has been sexually assaulted during their time there," President Obama said in January. Obama has cited the statistic multiple times throughout the last few years, as have Vice President Biden and the U.S. Department of Education. Senators use the statistic when writing legislation or holding hearings. Pundits and columnists have opened many an editorial with it, and it's a favorite of student activists, frequently appearing on hand-written signs at protests and marches.

For many it's a number that has helped galvanize a movement—an encapsulation of just how large the problem of campus sexual assault is. But for others, including some sexual assault prevention advocates and some who question the current focus on sexual assault on campus, the statistic can be a distraction, a lightning rod that generates more arguments than solutions and overshadows other research on the topic.

And many question just how accurate the figure is. John Foubert, founder of the sexual assault prevention group One in Four, said the proliferation of one in five "drives him nuts."

"It's so widespread because the of the Obama administration's use of it," he said. "I think they probably got some bad advice about which stat to cite because there are more reliable stats out there. The one in five statistic, it's from reputable researchers and a reputable study, but you can't really use those findings to generalize the whole United States."

That's because the statistic comes from a 2007 study that is based on a survey of just two colleges. Funded by the National Institute of Justice, the "Campus Sexual Assault Study" summarizes the online survey results of male and female students at two large public institutions. Nineteen percent, or about one in five, of the female respondents said they had experienced an attempted or completed sexual assault since starting college.

Defining Sexual Assault

Other critics have focused not so much on the limited scope of the survey, but rather its broad definition of sexual assault, which includes kissing and groping. The study's definition of sexual assault includes both rape—described as oral, anal, and vaginal penetration—and sexual battery, which was described as "sexual contact only, such as forced kissing and fondling." Some argue that an unwanted kiss should not be conflated with other kinds of more severe sexual assault or rape.

A version of that debate recently appeared on ABC's "This Week with George Stephanopoulos" during a discussion about *Rolling Stone's* article about sexual assault at the University of Virginia. When CNN's Van Jones mentioned the one in five statistic, Rich Lowry, editor of the *National Review,* interrupted [him] to call the stat "bogus."

"That statistic is based on a survey that includes attempted forced kissing as sexual assault," Lowry said. "That is not a real number."

"Can I kiss you?" Jones replied. "Can I kiss you here against your will? That's an assault. That is a sexual assault."

Laura Dunn, executive director of sexual assault prevention group SurvJustice, said the fact that some people still balk at the idea of unwanted kissing being considered sexual assault is a result of the criminal justice system frequently focusing on only the worst kinds of sexual violence. It's caused a particular image of sexual assault to form in people's heads, she said, and it's an image that denies a much broader expanse of offenses.

"People who deny this issue don't believe something like an unwanted kiss is harmful, but it is," Dunn said. "I think there's an idea in our society that says if a man's not using a gun or beating a woman, then it's O.K. to be pushy and aggressive, or to wait until she's drunk. We really think of some sexual aggression as really not that bad, and that mentality extends to the survivors as well. In these surveys, if you use broader legal terms, you actually get less reporting."

Indeed, when a survey doesn't include specific examples of what researchers mean by rape and sexual assault, the rate of sexual assault is much lower because many survey respondents, she said, don't immediately recognize the seriousness of what has happened.

A report released last week by the Bureau of Justice Statistics and based on the National Crime Victimization Survey, found that the rate for sexual assault among college women is 6.1 in 1,000.

If one in five is considered by some to overestimate the rate of sexual assault, the opposite is true for the NCVS numbers. Even the bureau itself has expressed doubts about the survey's ability to accurately count cases of sexual assault, and earlier this year it asked the National Research Council to look into the matter.

The council's conclusion: by using "ambiguous" words and phrases like "rape," the bureau is likely undercounting rape and sexual assault. Studies have repeatedly shown that many young women who are survivors of rape and sexual assault have trouble identifying it as such.

Similar Findings

Another point of confusion that surrounds "one in five," is what it's actually referring to. The original study suggests that one in five college women have experienced a completed or attempted sexual assault, again with a definition that covered just about any unwanted physical interaction of a sexual nature. The percentage of women in the study who specifically experienced completed sexual assaults was 13.7 percent. That some of the assaults were not actually completed is often omitted by pundits and politicians, but it's an important distinction, Dunn said.

"Only about one-third of campus rapes are completed," she said.

Despite the Campus Sexual Assault Study's shortcomings as a national barometer of the issue, other research has yielded similar findings—though with some caveats. A Centers for Disease Control and Prevention survey found that the rate of women who experience sexual assault is one in five, though that rate is for all women instead of just those going to college. That survey, too, has been questioned for its classification of having sex while intoxicated in any way as a sexual assault.

Then there's the statistic that gives John Foubert's organization its name: one in four. That comes from a Justice Department survey of 4,000 college women in 2006 that found that nearly one-quarter of college women have survived rape or attempted rape in their lifetime. While the study is of college women, the rape could have occurred at any point in their lives.

"I think it helps to have reliable statistics as it helps people understand how massive a problem this is," Foubert said. "It helps people realize that this is not just happening two or three times a year on a particular campus. This is widespread. I hope people would be concerned if this was even just happening once a year, but that fact is that it's happening far more than that, and we need reliable research to demonstrate that."

A national survey conducted by the Medical University of South Carolina in 2007 found that more than 12 percent of college women had been raped, not just sexually assaulted, which is about the same percentage of women in the one-in-five study who said they were raped. The researchers calculated that about 5 percent of college women are raped annually, an estimate that is backed up by separate research by the American College Health Association. That's about 300,000 female students raped every year, a vastly larger number than what the Bureau of Justice Statistics calculates. According to its new report, 30,000 college women were raped in 2013.

While 30,000 is a much smaller number than 300,000, many advocates say colleges should view even 30,000 as a terrible figure, representing far too many female students whose rights have been violated and whose well-being has been endangered, and one that should not be viewed as acceptable.

More research still needs to be done to get a better sense of just how prevalent campus sexual assault truly is, Dunn said, but she believes the few available numbers are already painting a bleak and clear enough picture.

"I believe in the one in five statistic wholeheartedly because I am a survivor and I remember how many of my friends disclosed that it had happened to them too," she said. "Most women don't doubt this statistic because we are aware in our conversations how common sexual violence is in our experience.

9

Sexual Assaults on Campuses Are Underreported or Not Reported At All

Kristen Lombardi

Kristen Lombardi is an award-winning journalist and senior reporter at the Center for Public Integrity. Her investigative work into campus rape cases won her the Robert F. Kennedy Award, the Dart Award, and the Sigma Delta Chi Award for Public Service, among other awards.

This investigative report finds that many schools don't even include sexual assaults on their annual security or crime reports. According to Lombardi, this is actually legal because of loopholes in the Clery Act, a federal mandatory campus crime reporting law. According to some watchdogs, schools are intentionally underreporting sexual assaults on campus in order to protect the reputations of their campuses. But that's not the only reason. Schools also ignore or refuse to address sexual assault cases and, just as troubling, only an estimated 5 percent of students who experience rape report it to school officials.

Asexual assault prevention program documented 46 sexual assaults at West Virginia University in a recent academic year. But those 46 incidents didn't show up in the university's annual security report.

A counseling and victim advocacy program at the University of Iowa served 62 students, faculty, and staff who reported being

"Campus Sexual Assault Statistics Don't Add Up," by Kristen Lombardi, Center for Public Integrity, December 2, 2009. Reprinted by permission.

raped or almost raped in the last fiscal year. Those incidents didn't show up, either.

A victim advocate program at Florida State University compiled statistics on 57 sexual offenses both on and off campus in 2008. Only a fraction of those incidents appeared in the school's official crime statistics.

Across the higher education community, such discrepancies are not unusual. A nine-month investigation by The Center for Public Integrity has found that limitations and loopholes in the federal mandatory campus crime reporting law, known as the Clery Act, are causing systematic problems in accurately documenting the total numbers of campus-related sexual assaults. The most troubling of these loopholes involves broadly applied reporting exemptions for counselors who may be covered by confidentiality protections. Confusion over definitions of sexual offenses, as well as the law's comprehensive reporting provisions, have created additional problems. "When you talk to 10 different institutions," explains Marlon Lynch, president of the International Association of Campus Law Enforcement Administrators, "you almost find 10 different ways of reporting under the law."

Available data suggest that, on many campuses, far more sexual offenses are occurring than are reflected in the official Clery numbers. A Center survey of 152 crisis-services programs and clinics on or near college campuses requested incident numbers over the past year: 58 facilities responded with hard statistics. Clery totals from higher education institutions are theoretically supposed to include information from such service providers, but confusion remains over exactly who must report. A comparison of the survey data with the schools' previous five-year average of official Clery totals shows that the clinic numbers are considerably higher, suggesting a systematic problem with Clery data collection.

Responses to the Center's survey found that 49 out of those 58 crisis-services programs and clinics recorded higher reports of sexual offenses in a recent one-year period than the average yearly figure submitted by their schools in Clery statistics from 2002 to

2006—the last five years for which full Clery data are available. At Florida State University, for instance, those 57 sexual assaults logged by the victim advocacy program are more than double the university's average 26 sexual offenses recorded from 2002 to 2006.

Some of the discrepancies are explainable. Many clinics record higher statistics because they serve a broader clientele than the schools' student populations or because some of the incidents occurred elsewhere—particularly off campus. And crisis counselors say they routinely document reports from students who were sexually assaulted on spring break, raped in high school, or molested as children—none of which fall under Clery reporting requirements. But many survey respondents affirmed assertions from critics that colleges and universities are ducking bad publicity by exploiting weaknesses in the Clery Act and ignoring their clinic numbers, thus keeping official statistics low.

"Clery, in our minds, doesn't do what it was intended to do," says Mary Friedrichs of the Office of Victim Assistance at the University of Colorado at Boulder. The 42 sexual assaults documented by her program in one recent year didn't appear in the university's Clery data because, as certified counselors with confidentiality exemptions, her staff doesn't report them to the campus police. By comparison, CU recorded an average of 14 sexual offenses from 2002 to 2006. Echoing many victim advocates, Friedrichs adds, "We don't think it [the official data] tells a story that is understandable."

Clery Confusion

The Clery Act requires some 7,500 colleges and universities—nearly 4,000 of which are four-year public and private institutions—to disclose statistics about crime on or near their campuses in annual security reports. Many provisions have evolved since the law passed 19 years ago, but what hasn't changed is Clery's requirement that schools poll a wide range of "campus security authorities" when gathering data. That designation includes a broad array of campus programs, departments, and centers, such as student health centers, women's centers, and even counseling centers. The designation also applies to officials who supervise students—deans, coaches, housing directors, judicial affairs officers, to name a few. Experts on the law say that any center or program set up by an institution to respond to crime victims and to serve their needs should be designated a campus security authority, requiring Clery reporting. Only licensed mental-health and pastoral counselors are explicitly exempt from Clery reporting requirements.

In theory, those stipulations should make for comprehensive crime reporting. At the University of Iowa, a compliance team, led by the public safety department, collects documentation from non-police campus authorities and compiles statistics. According to Associate Dean of Students Tom Baker, who oversaw the process for years, the university distributes an e-mail letter seeking key details on sexual assaults and other crimes reported to campus authorities in a half-dozen offices and programs, including the school's sexual misconduct response coordinator. The law requires schools to solicit information from local police departments, and Iowa's team contacts four of them.

But the data gathering isn't always meticulous. In fact, a 2002 study funded by the U.S. Department of Justice found that "only 36.5 percent of schools reported crime statistics in a manner that was fully consistent with the Clery Act." A Center examination of 10 years worth of complaints filed against institutions under Clery shows that the most common problem is that schools are not properly collecting data. Some submit only reports from law-enforcement officials. In August 2004, Yale University became the subject of a complaint after it was discovered to be doing just that. Five years later, the U.S. Department of Education has yet to finish its review; a department spokesperson declined to comment on the pending inquiry. Evidently, though, the complaint has sparked some changes. Peter Parker, who heads Yale's sexual harassment grievance board, began forwarding sexual assault data to the school's official Clery reporter in 2007. "Before that," he confirms, "nobody had asked us to compile our reports."

Other schools submit inaccurate sexual assault statistics—in some cases inadvertently; in others cases, intentionally. Nearly half of the 25 Clery complaint investigations conducted by the Education Department over the past decade determined that schools were omitting sexual offenses collected by some sources or failing to report them at all. In October 2007, the department fined LaSalle University, in Philadelphia, $110,000 for not reporting 28 crimes, including a small number of sexual assaults. (The university appealed the decision and then settled for $87,500, without admitting it was at fault.) In April 2005, Salem International University, in West Virginia, agreed to pay the department $200,000 in fines after never reporting a sexual offense in its Clery reports, even though the school itself had documented such offenses.

There's also been misclassification of sexual assaults. Schools can wrongly categorize reports of acquaintance rape or fondling as "non-forcible" sexual offenses—a definition that should only apply to incest and statutory rape. Five of the 25 Clery audits found schools were miscoding forcible rapes as non-forcible instead. In June 2008, Eastern Michigan University agreed to pay the department $350,000—the largest Clery fine ever—for a host of violations, including miscoding rapes. In February 2002, officials determined that Mount Saint Mary College, in New York, had incorrectly reported two sexual offenses as non-forcible; the school had to correct the error. The problem has grown so prevalent that the department now calls schools whenever they submit even one report of a non-forcible sexual offense.

"I don't know anyone who's read the definitions [who] can claim there are any non-forcible sex offenses on campuses," says David Bergeron of the department's Office of Postsecondary Education, which monitors Clery compliance. Still, 27 colleges reported one or two non-forcible sex offenses in their 2006 Clery data.

School officials and watchdog groups agree that colleges have improved Clery reporting over the past two decades. Dolores Stafford, police chief at George Washington University and a national expert on the Clery Act, has trained campus police officers and administrators on the law since the late 1990s, and has seen what she calls "a sea change" in attitudes, which she attributes to improved training and guidance from the Education Department. These days, she says, "There are less intentional and egregious violators." Department audits still reveal schools getting in trouble over their data, she explains, "but not a whole lot of areas where people are purposely underreporting or over-reporting."

Are the Numbers Believable?

Indeed, today's issues may be subtler than that. Rape generally ranks among the most underreported of all crime statistics, experts say. But critics point out that the huge percentage of schools reporting no incidents whatsoever indicates a serious problem with Clery data collection. In 2006, in fact, 3,068 two- and four-year colleges and universities—77 percent—reported zero sexual offenses. Another 501 reported just one or two.

All those miniscule totals look like red flags to watchdog organizations. "Find any school with a zero, and you'll find problems with Clery reporting," asserts Margaret Jakobson, a victims' advocate who's testified before Congress about issues with Clery compliance. In the late '90s, Jakobson, along with Security on Campus, a watchdog group, filed some of the earliest Clery Act complaints after identifying students who had reported being raped on campuses touting zeros.

"It strains believability to think that those numbers could actually be true," says Mark Goodman, former director of the Student Press Law Center, which has long lobbied to close Clery loopholes. He, like many critics, suspects that some schools are intentionally misinterpreting their obligations under Clery and weeding out reports in order to protect their reputations as safe campuses.

But Lynch, of the law enforcement administrators, and other campus police chiefs believe all those zeros most likely reflect something else: Most rape victims don't report the crime in the first place. The 2002 Justice Department-funded study has actually pegged the number of college women who report their rapes to campus police or other officials at just under five percent. It could be that some schools with low sexual assault statistics don't do a good job at encouraging student victims to come forward. Or it could be that some do—and still end up with zeros. After all, one limitation of the Clery Act is that statistics reflect "official" reports. In other words, a victim has to tell a campus security authority for a sexual assault to count.

"We get the feeling that people would prefer that we would report a lot of sexual assaults even if we were making it up," observes Stafford, the George Washington chief, "but I can only report what I know."

Another limitation of the Clery Act: it counts only those crimes occurring on or near campuses, and in school-affiliated buildings like fraternity houses. The initial thinking behind this narrow geographic focus was that off-campus crimes would inevitably be documented by local police, experts say. But that means that Clery statistics don't include such settings as off-campus apartments, where most campus-related rapes are believed to take place. Last year, Jacqui Pequignot, who heads the victim advocate program at Florida State, recorded just nine sexual offenses on or near campus, as compared to 48 off campus. Pequignot, who estimates that 36,000 of FSU's 42,000 students live in apartments more than a block from the university, notes that critics often suspect misreporting whenever they don't see huge numbers of campus sexual assaults. "But sometimes," she says, "it's really just about the fact that the numbers are greater off campus."

See No Evil

Some schools ignore the reports of sexual assaults they do have. At the University of Iowa, alleged victims are instructed to contact the Rape Victim Advocacy Program for medical and counseling services. Housed on campus, the advocacy program records all calls, and categorizes incidents on or off campus. But these numbers don't appear in the university's security report, confirms associate counsel Rob Porter, because certified counselors make up the staff—and they have that privacy exemption. Instead, the school explains in a report footnote that the advocacy program has its own statistics.

And that's more than what some schools do with counselors' reports. At Texas Tech University, counselors don't track the details of an alleged assault—its time, its location—needed for Clery reporting purposes. Jack Floyd, who compiles the Clery data, says counselors are encouraged to forward information about sexual assaults and other crimes to campus police. But, he affirms, "Nobody has returned a report form since I've been here," beginning in 2001.

"Confidentiality inhibits our requirement to do so," says Eileen Nathan, of the Texas Tech counseling center, explaining why the staff do not submit reports.

In fact, some counselors believe the fine print of the Clery Act encourages them not to report. Under the law, licensed therapists and pastoral counselors are the only campus employees excluded from reporting requirements. Schools can still use aggregate information—minus names and other identifying information—on sexual assaults from counseling centers, experts say. And interviews with survey respondents reveal that some colleges designate a center staffer as a campus authority for Clery purposes. Others offer a blanket exemption to the entire counseling staff, however, fueling criticisms that administrators are merely exploiting a loophole to keep official statistics low. Even Education Department officials suggest as much.

"Some institutions may try to stretch that [counselor] privilege," Bergeron says.

One of the schools that has faced controversy on that front is West Virginia University. Deb Beazley is the sexual assault prevention educator at WVU; she is not a licensed counselor. Beazley helps alleged victims navigate services and heads the countywide sexual assault response team that services the campus. She maintains what she calls a "universal reporting system" of incidents culled from her records, as well as from university faculty and staff. She classifies the anonymous, third-party reports based on incident date, time, and location, either on or off campus. She even records the birth date of alleged victims to avoid double-counting. By all accounts, she compiles numbers in a way that would satisfy Clery requirements. But they don't end up in official data, as per school policy, even though West Virginia counts rape reports forwarded to campus police by non-police campus authorities.

"It's important to understand that, by definition, what Deb is collecting is survey data," explains Bob Roberts, police chief at West Virginia University, "and we do not take survey data because it is anonymous."

Roberts is not a stranger to Clery reporting disputes; in March 2004, West Virginia became the subject of a Clery Act complaint after three whistleblower police officers alleged that the university was miscoding crimes. Last September, the Education Department found some problems with the way the university had dealt with sexual assaults—misclassifying forcible and non-forcible offenses, and failing to include sexual assault reports. In its response to the department's preliminary findings, dated October 30, 2008, the university admitted the errors and outlined recent steps to bolster its record-keeping. But counting Beazley's anonymous reports isn't among the improvements.

"You have to compare apples to apples," contends Roberts, who now trains campus officials around the state on the finer points of the Clery Act, "and other campuses I know of are not reporting anonymous data."

Yet some schools clearly are—Florida State, for one. Experts say colleges should count numbers from any campus program set up for victims to report crimes and seek services. Stafford, the George Washington chief, collects statistics from her university's response team, its counseling center, and its health center in order to "give people a full picture of what's happening on the campus." Still, she stresses that schools ignoring these numbers are not necessarily violating the law.

"It is not clear in the [Education Department's Clery Act] handbook or in the law ... that victim advocates and sexual assault services coordinators are required to report," she says. "It's a big weakness right now."

And one not likely to change any time soon. According to Bergeron, the Education Department has to allow some room for schools to interpret who actually constitutes a campus security authority; after all, it has to regulate everything from a for-profit technical school to a four-year university. He doubts it's possible to write a department regulation answering "every question in every circumstance that everyone on a campus would ever encounter," he adds.

But there's little doubt that the differing interpretations of the law are sowing confusion—with one school submitting sexual assault statistics beyond what's required and another the bare minimum. Ultimately, these loopholes, coupled with the law's limitations, can render Clery data almost meaningless. Victim advocates point out that the schools they believe are reporting the most accurate sexual assault numbers—the 10 percent who reported three or more rapes in 2006—now have to compete with all those schools touting zeros.

"It's almost like UMass gets penalized for doing it correctly," notes Rebecca Lockwood, who heads rape crisis services at the University of Massachusetts Amherst, where her program numbers are gathered for Clery purposes. In 2006, UMass Amherst ranked among just 61 schools, or 1.5 percent, documenting campus sexual assaults in the double digits. As Lockwood sees it, "I'd like to see the schools that report zero be held accountable."

10

Students Must Fight Back Against Sexual Violence on Campus

Gaylynn Burroughs and Debra S. Katz

Gaylynn Burroughs is the policy director for the advocacy organization the Feminist Majority Foundation. Debra S. Katz is a civil rights lawyer who specializes in Title IX cases. She is currently working with Feminists United in their case against the University of Mary Washington.

In 2015, student activists at the University of Mary Washington (UMW) filed a complaint against their university, arguing that UMW disregarded Title IX, a federal statute that prohibits sex discrimination in education. When a group of students associated with the campus group Feminists United rallied against rape culture on campus, they were harassed by other campus groups, including fraternities, who threatened them with rape. Voicing their concerns to UMV officials, the students were told that such threats were protected by the First Amendment. In this viewpoint, feminist policy director Gaylynn Burroughs and civil rights lawyer Debra S. Katz recount the students' fight for their rights on campus.

This spring, instead of celebrating finishing up her final exams, Julia Michels stood on the steps of George Washington Hall, in the heart of the University of Mary Washington's Fredericksburg, Virginia, campus, to announce the filing of a Title IX complaint against her school.

"Won't Back down," by Gaylynn Burroughs & Debra Katz, www.feminist.org, Summer 2015. Reprinted by permission of Ms. magazine, © 2015.

Speaking in the same spot where, just a few months earlier, a crowd of students rallied to demand an end to rape culture on campus, Michels, the incoming president of Feminists United, recounted her group's efforts to push the university to protect them from threats of rape and violence, and other forms of sexist cyber-harassment they'd faced regularly on Yik Yak, an anonymous social media app popular on many college campuses.

Feminists United members became the target of hundreds of abusive Yaks after they spoke out against sexual assault on their campus and at other schools. "I have never before experienced anxiety and fear on the same level I did during this last year," said Michels. She explained that her grades and schoolwork suffered because of the abuse, and that other students had suffered emotional or psychological harm. They all agreed: The university had betrayed them through inaction.

Students at UMW and across the fed up with inaction from university officials, are taking matters into their own hands. A massive movement has resulted in a flood of Title IX complaints and the creation of new federal rules to strengthen efforts on college campuses to prevent sexual violence and hold perpetrators accountable. These efforts have led to real change on some campuses, but students are not relying solely on universities or the Department of Education to protect their rights. Instead, they are pursuing justice through a variety of avenues, including the courts.

The problem at the University of Mary Washington began when then president of Feminists United, Paige McKinsey, opposed official recognition of fraternities at UMW and later published an op-ed in the student newspaper decrying rape culture on campus; she criticized members of the school's rugby team who'd been recorded chanting about rape and necrophilia. Yik Yak exploded with vitriol. Anonymous posters referred to Feminists United members as "feminazis" and "femicunts." Other posts, Michels recalls, charged that Feminists United was a "hate group" on a "witch hunt." Some of the posts included physical and sexual threats, including references to rape and euthanasia. Yakkers even posted

McKinsey's whereabouts so people could "call her out in person," encouraging potentially threatening confrontations. McKinsey became so frightened she asked campus police to accompany her to student group meetings.

"I was terrified," explained Michels. "I did not know if the person sitting next to me in class had just threatened to hurt me anonymously, and I had no way to gauge the seriousness of these threats."

Feminists United alerted the university and requested that it take action. Instead, the UMW Title IX coordinator sent an email to the student body stating that "the university had no recourse for such cyberbullying" and directing the students to take their complaints to Yik Yak directly. Michels emailed the Title IX coordinator to express frustration that the university was shirking its legal obligations. "It should not be the responsibility of students to prevent their own bullying, or to address threats aimed against them," she wrote. "We ask that the university itself be the one to take the lead against this problem."

The university, however, continued to do little more than say the issue was "complicated" and cite apprehensions about the First Amendment. But the school's concerns are misguided. As long ago as 1969, the Supreme Court found that schools do not violate First Amendment rights when they regulate or restrict student speech that interferes materially and substantially with the operation of the school or infringes on the rights of other students. "Freedom of speech does not extend to harassment that creates a hostile environment or to threats of violence," says Shireen Mitchell, founder of Digital Sisters/Sistas. "There is no right to threaten someone's life with impunity, whether in-person or online."

Title IX of the education amendments of 1972 prohibits sex discrimination in education programs or activities that receive federal funding. The law has been a game changer for women. Before Title IX, less than 15 percent of women ages 25 to 34 held a bachelor's degree or higher. Today, women are more likely to go to college than men and more likely to graduate. "We fought tirelessly to get women into college and graduate programs," said Feminist Majority Foundation President (and publisher of *Ms.*) Eleanor Smeal. "Now, we're fighting to make sure that they aren't pushed out by sexual violence, harassment and discrimination."

Title IX provides one tool for doing just that. In addition to dismantling barriers to entry into educational institutions, Title IX obligates schools— both public and private—receiving federal funds to remedy and prevent sexual violence and discrimination whether or not the harassing behavior occurs in person or online. A university's failure to act violates students' civil rights.

The complaint against UMW, filed on behalf of Feminists United, a Feminist Majority Foundation campus affiliate, and others, alleges that the school violated Title IX by failing to protect students from a sexually hostile environment, sex-based cyber assaults, and threats of physical and sexual violence. It is one of the first complaints to arise from a university's failure to adequately address the creation of a sexually hostile environment fueled by anonymous social media. According to a Pew Research Center study, around 70 percent of young adults who use the Internet have been the targets of online harassment, and young women are disproportionately affected. Other studies show that people of color are also frequent targets of abuse: Around 51 percent of African American and 54 percent of Hispanic Internet users report experiencing harassment, compared to 34 percent of whites. The epidemic of campus sexual violence—both online and off— is indisputably nationwide, affecting small and large campuses, public and private universities, religiously affiliated colleges and everything in between.

Title IX legally obligates schools to investigate sexual harassment and discrimination on campus. Under the law, once a school knows, or should know, about an incident of sex discrimination, it must promptly investigate what occurred and immediately remedy the situation. The Campus Sexual Violence Elimination Act (Campus SaVE) bolstered Title IX by requiring schools to create prevention programs and clarifying schools' obligations to make survivors aware of their reporting options. Campus SaVE also strengthened the Jeanne Clery Act, which requires colleges and universities receiving federal funds to report and publicize crime statistics annually, and to alert the campus of known public safety risks. The range of crimes schools must disclose now includes domestic and dating violence, stalking and sexual assault. Administrations that fail to comply could face a $35,000 fine for each violation.

These policy changes would not have been possible without the work of student activists and recent graduates, along with national groups such as the American Association of University Women, Feminist Majority Foundation, Legal Momentum and the National Women's Law Center, which pushed to make this issue a national priority.

Activists from Know Your IX and End Rape on Campus have not only fought for legislative change, but have also developed networks to help students file Title IX complaints with the Department of Education to hold college administrations accountable for failing to appropriately address sexual assault. Other networks, such as Black Women's Blueprint and Carry That Weight, are demanding better policies on campus and stronger implementation to end gender-based violence and counter rape culture.

Their efforts have been supported by the Obama administration, which has issued guidance to help schools comply with Title IX. The administration also launched a White House Task Force to Protect Students from Sexual Assault, leading to the creation of NotAlone.gov, a website where students and school administrators can find resources on Title IX, including legal advice and a guide for drafting sexual-misconduct policies.

The torrent of activity at both the national and campus levels has correlated with an exponential rise in the number of Title IX complaints received by the Department of Education Office of Civil Rights (OCR). Between 2009 and 2014, sexual-violence complaints at higher education institutions increased by more than 1,000 percent. This increase, together with a lack of appropriate resources, has contributed to severe delays in the resolution of complaints. In May, OCR reported that the average duration of a sexual-violence investigation in 2015 was 940 days, or more than two years.

Schools that are ultimately found to violate Title IX may lose federal funding. Although no school has faced this penalty yet, termination of funding is not an empty threat, something Tufts University learned last year after attempting to back out of a voluntary compliance agreement it entered into with OCR. Tufts was found to have failed to adequately investigate or address student complaints of sexual assault and harassment and specifically failed to protect the complainant from a hostile environment. The agreement required the school to revise its policies, procedures and investigative practices concerning complaints of sexual assault and harassment.

Less than 10 days later, Tufts notified OCR that it was revoking the agreement. OCR subsequently issued a press release informing the school that it "may move to initiate proceedings to terminate federal funding of Tufts." Tufts eventually recommitted to the agreement and announced the creation of a "response and resource coordinator" to assist student-survivors in accessing needed services.

Given delays in investigating Title IX complaints and the limited relief offered by OCR, students should know that there are other avenues available to vindicate their civil rights. Some student-survivors have initiated their own private lawsuits against universities, with a few high-profile cases settling out of court. Survivors have been able to obtain large settlements and create change.

In one case, a student sued the University of Colorado at Boulder after she reported being sexually assaulted at a party by football players and recruits. The suit alleged that the university knew that several students had been assaulted over a period of years during alcohol-fueled parties meant to entertain football recruits on school-sponsored campus visits. The university agreed to pay $2.5 million to settle the suit and hired an independent

Title IX adviser as well as a counselor for its Office of Victim Assistance. In the wake of the lawsuit, several university staff and administrators—including the president, chancellor, athletic director and football coach—resigned.

In a 2014 case, the University of Connecticut settled a Title IX lawsuit brought by five survivors for over $1.2 million; students alleged that UConn had failed to respond appropriately to reports of rape and threatening behavior. One woman who reported to campus police that she'd been raped, for example, says she was told, "Women have to just stop spreading their legs like peanut butter," or else rape is going to "keep on happening till the cows come home." UConn did not admit any wrongdoing in the settlement, but the lawsuit did lead to several changes, including the creation of a Special Victims Unit within campus police, increased training of university staff and more resources for the Office of the Title IX Coordinator.

Monetary settlements are important for survivors. These students often suffer economic harm, including lost tuition and student aid, and expenses related to counseling, tutoring and new housing. And the settlements may help student-survivors in future cases attract quality legal representation. Universities and fraternities have long had a cadre of lawyers and lobbyists ready to protect their financial interests, but student-survivors haven't had that same advantage. Additionally, students may find that universities forced to pay for failing to comply with Title IX are much more likely to take student claims seriously in order to avoid liability.

In their documentary *The Hunting Ground*, filmmakers Kirby Dick and Amy Ziering expose how colleges and universities systematically cover up incidents of sexual violence. The film focuses on the business side of educational institutions, demonstrating how schools are motivated by money, reputation loss and liability when making decisions about how to handle reports of sexual assault. It also shows how money and power allow athletic teams and fraternities to achieve an almost untouchable status at some universities.

Just this past spring, the Fraternity and Sorority Political Action Committee, or FratPAC, which has helped raise millions for federal candidates, planned on lobbying Congress for a requirement that would prevent universities from investigating sexual-assault allegations until cases were resolved by the criminal justice system. Days before students were to arrive on Capitol Hill, and after nationwide criticism from students, including many Greeks, the organizers announced they would postpone their efforts.

FratPAC's proposal would not only have violated Title IX, it would have prevented schools from addressing sexual violence on campus unless a student filed a police report, a measure that would drastically reduce the ability of campuses to respond at all. According to a 2007 report, only 12 percent of college-student survivors report to the police, with male survivors reporting at lower rates than women. Even when students do report, resolving a criminal complaint could take years.

Rape and sexual assault are serious crimes under state and federal laws, and the criminal justice system should be an ally for survivors, especially since most rapists are repeat offenders. Yet law enforcement has been notorious for failing to properly investigate sexual assault, and some universities have actively repelled local law enforcement, obstructing the ability of police to investigate crimes; for instance, police have been refused access to some campuses when attempting to serve orders of protection or to interview alleged perpetrators.

"The campus system cannot adequately ensure the safety of the community beyond the college borders," explained Laura Dunn, a former University of Wisconsin student activist, sexual-assault survivor and founder of SurvJustice. "Knowing your rights and options in every system—and having proper legal support to navigate them all—is essential for survivors to truly be safe and demand accountability after sexual violence."

There is clearly much more work to be done to reduce sexual violence and harassment on college campuses—but student activists are not giving up. After Feminists United filed its Title IX complaint against UMW, university president Richard Hurley sent a hostile and disparaging letter to FMF President Eleanor Smeal, the entire UMW community and the media. Members of Feminists United responded with a strong statement of their own, blasting President Hurley for his misrepresentation of the complaint. "Worse still," they wrote, "the way you framed the conversation about these threats, suggesting that members of our club were somewhat at fault for opening themselves up to criticism, was eerily similar to the victim blaming that is so prominent in rape culture."

The students later amended their Title IX complaint to add a retaliation claim against the university. "We're not backing down," said Julia Michels.

Michels realizes that the complaint will probably not be resolved while she is a student at UMW. That fact does not dampen her determination. "We care about other students," she said. "We have hope that the environment will improve, and we want to make it better for the people who will come after us."

Asked if she had any advice for other students wanting to organize their campuses, Michels said, "Remember that there are people who can help. Reach out to professors, national organizations, community groups and other student associations. Keep fighting. Don't give up. Show them you are not going away."

11

The College Judicial System Leaves Rape Victims Feeling Victimized Again

Kristen Lombardi

Kristen Lombardi is an award-winning journalist and senior reporter at the Center for Public Integrity. Her investigative work into campus rape cases won her the Robert F. Kennedy Award, the Dart Award, and the Sigma Delta Chi Award for Public Service, among other awards.

In this investigative piece, Lombardi examines how universities tackle reports of sexual assault on their campuses. Unfortunately, she finds that reporting sexual assault leads to a labyrinth of closed hearings, confusing laws, and stringent (if not illegal) "gag orders" never to talk about the attack again. While universities view it necessary to protect their brand, survivors of sexual assault on campus feel their treatment by their own schools upon coming forward constitutes a double betrayal. By trying to speak out for their own rights, many student victims of sexual assault feel as though they are being victimized all over again.

Three hours into deliberations by the University of Virginia's Sexual Assault Board, UVA junior Kathryn Russell sat with her mother in a closet-like room in sprawling Peabody Hall. Down the corridor, two professors and two students were deciding her fate. Russell was replaying in her mind, endlessly, details of her allegations of rape when, she remembers, Shamim Sisson, the

"Sexual Assault on Campus Shrouded in Secrecy," by Kristen Lombardi, Center for Public Integrity, December 1, 2009. Reprinted by permission.

board chair, stepped into the room and delivered the order: *You can't talk about the verdict to anyone.*

That stern admonition was a reminder of the silence Russell had been keeping since, she says, she struggled to break free from a fellow student's grip in her dorm. That's the account she gave local authorities, who declined to prosecute. And that's what, in May 2004, she told the UVA Sexual Assault Board, whose decision she'd considered "my last resort."

Russell stands among the tiny minority of students who have pursued rape complaints in the college judicial system—33 at UVA, a school of 21,057 students, since 1998. She became well-versed in the confidential nature of the process as described in the school's 2004 written procedures. Deans repeated the blanket stipulation to her "ad nauseam," she says, throughout her three-month proceeding. The school later defended its mandatory confidentiality policy before the U.S. Department of Education even while softening the language.

Relating the gag order back in the room, Sisson, Russell says, provided a strong incentive to keep quiet: *If you talk of the verdict, you'll face disciplinary charges.*

At the time, the exchange didn't faze Russell, who says she did as told in an effort to get justice. But five years later, she's come to see the school's old confidentiality policy as emblematic of just how far colleges and universities will go to keep secret cases of alleged sexual assault. And a recent ruling by the Education Department against UVA for a policy "inconsistent with the letter and spirit" of the law has resulted in significant changes there.

Silent Victims, Secretive Administrators

But an array of practices at UVA and college campuses elsewhere continues to shroud the college judicial system in controversy. Indeed, a nine-month investigation by the Center for Public Integrity has found that a thick blanket of secrecy still envelops cases involving allegations of sexual assault on campus. One national study reports that roughly one in five women who attend college will become the victim of a rape or an attempted rape by the time she graduates. But while the vast majority of students who are sexually assaulted remain silent—just over 95 percent, according to a study funded by the research arm of the U.S. Justice Department—those who come forward can encounter mystifying disciplinary proceedings, secretive school administrations, and off-the-record negotiations. At times, policies lead to dropped complaints and, in cases like Russell's, gag orders later found to be illegal. Many college administrators believe the existing processes provide a fair and effective way to deal with ultra-sensitive allegations, but alleged victims say these processes leave them feeling like victims a second time.

The Center has interviewed 48 experts familiar with the disciplinary process—student affairs administrators, conduct hearing officers, assault services directors, victim advocates—as well as 33 female students who have reported being raped by other students. The inquiry has included a review of records in select cases, and examinations of 10 years worth of complaints filed against institutions with the U.S. Education Department under Title IX and the Clery Act—two laws requiring schools to respond to assault claims and to offer key rights to alleged victims. The Center has also surveyed 152 crisis-services programs and clinics on or near college campuses nationwide over the past year.

Just over half the students interviewed by the Center have reported they unsuccessfully sought criminal charges and instead had to seek justice in closed, school-run administrative proceedings that led either to academic penalties or no punishment at all for their alleged assailants, leaving them feeling betrayed by a process they say has little transparency or accountability. Some of those students, including Russell, said they were ordered to keep quiet about the proceedings and threatened with punishment if they did not. Still other students said administrators discouraged them from pursuing rape complaints. Survey respondents indicated similar problems with the closed procedures on campuses.

Undoubtedly, another law, the Family Educational Rights and Privacy Act, complicates the issue. FERPA forbids schools from divulging students' educational records, including disciplinary records. Administrators believe it binds them to silence on case details, but others aren't so sure. Under FERPA, colleges *can* release names of students found "responsible" for committing violent acts. But "we don't," concedes Rick Olshak, associate dean of students at Illinois State University, "and I don't know anyone who does, frankly." Victim advocates contend that colleges use the law as a smokescreen to cover up campus crimes.

"Most institutions have a strong interest in keeping sexual assaults as quiet as possible," says David Lisak, an associate professor at the University of Massachusetts- Boston, who has trained college administrators on combating sexual violence. Typically, Lisak notes, administrators view campus sexual assault as "a very negative piece of publicity," tarnishing institutional reputations, and heightening fears among tuition-paying parents and students for whom colleges are aggressively competing.

College administrators bristle at the idea they're shielding rapes. But they admit they've wrestled with confidentiality in campus assault proceedings because of FERPA and the Clery Act. Confusion over the laws has reinforced what critics see as a culture of silence that casts doubt on the credibility of the process. "People will think we're running star chambers," says Don Gehring, founder of the Association for Student Conduct Administration, referring to secret, arbitrary courts in old England. "And that's what's happening now."

Kathryn Russell's Allegations

Russell first approached the UVA administration in February 2004. UVA is required by Title IX regulations to respond "promptly and equitably" when a student alleges sexual assault—investigating the claim and taking action to eliminate harm. Most institutions, including UVA, list "sexual assault" or "sexual misconduct" as prohibited acts in their official standards of conduct—allegations of which automatically trigger internal disciplinary processes.

A petite, perky student who counted herself "a nerd," Russell reported that she had been raped on February 13 by a fellow junior whom she'd gotten to know through a class and a club the year before. On a campus prone to what UVA assault-services director Claire Kaplan calls "a culture of silence around sexual assault," administrators say they have strived to encourage reporting. "We try to make it clear that UVA ... has zero tolerance for sexual offenders," says Patricia Lampkin, vice president for student affairs, "and that students need to report all assaults." In 2004, Russell became one of eight to recount an alleged rape in a UVA dorm.

Eight days after filing an incident report; after telling UVA police she had "unwanted sexual contact"; after informing UVA doctors of "worsening pain" from allegedly forced sex, Russell found herself repeating the story to Penny Rue, then dean of students. The dean gave Russell a 12-page document, entitled "UNIVERSITY OF VIRGINIA PROCEDURES FOR SEXUAL ASSAULT CASES," which outlined options for adjudicating complaints. It included this language:

Confidentiality of the hearings process is of great importance to all involved. Identity of the reporting or accused student and any formal discipline resulting from the hearing may not be publicly disclosed....

Rue didn't dwell on the policy at first. Instead, Russell remembers the dean doing what many victim advocates say is common: discouraging her from pursuing a hearing. Rue, Russell charges, recommended mediation—an equally shrouded process in which, according to the UVA procedures, "all verbal statements ... must remain confidential," including "offers of apologies and concessions."

"I didn't want to talk to him," recalls Russell, of her alleged assailant, so mediation seemed out of the question. She would later initiate her complaint in a March 19 e-mail to Rue.

In ensuing days, the dean would informally "confront" Russell's alleged assailant, who claimed he'd had consensual sex with Russell. In his March 30, 2004, statement to UVA administrators, the accused student portrayed Russell as a willing flirt at a bar who turned sexual aggressor in her dorm, and who repeatedly "grabbed my genitals and wanted me not to leave." The individual in question did not respond to multiple calls, e-mails, and letters from the Center seeking comment.

Rue now works as vice chancellor of student affairs at the University of California, San Diego. In an August 2005 letter addressed to UVA's associate general counsel, obtained by the Center for Public Integrity, Rue confirmed meeting Russell and handing her the school's written procedures. The dean said she'd been careful to lay out all the options. "I let her know that it was her decision whether to pursue charges," Rue wrote in the letter, "and that the University would support her either way." Rue declined to discuss Russell's case with the Center, as did other former and current UVA officials familiar with it, despite a waiver from Russell granting permission for them to do so.

Informal Proceedings Common

Days before filing her complaint, Russell learned that the local district attorney wouldn't press criminal charges—a typical outcome. Experts say the reasons are simple: Most cases involving campus rape allegations come down to he-said-she-said accounts of sexual acts that clearly occurred; they lack independent corroboration like physical evidence or eyewitness testimony. At times, alcohol and drugs play such a central role, students can't remember details. Given all this, says Gary Pavela, who ran judicial programs at the University of Maryland, College Park, "A prosecutor says, 'I'm not going to take this to a jury.'" Often, the only venues in which to resolve these cases are on campus.

Internal disciplinary panels, like the UVA Sexual Assault Board, exist in various forms on most campuses. But they're not the only way schools handle rape allegations. For decades, informal proceedings run by an administrator have represented the most common method to adjudicate disciplinary matters. Typically, an administrator meets with both students, separately, in an attempt to resolve a complaint. Occasionally, they "mediate" the incident. Officials find such adjudication appealing in uncontested situations. If a dean elicits a confession, says Olshak, of Illinois State, who headed the student conduct association in 2001, "We'll be able to resolve the complaint quickly, easily, and without the confrontation of a judicial hearing." Resolution, as in formal hearings, can mean expulsion, suspension, probation, or another academic penalty, like an assigned research paper. By all accounts, informal processes take place almost as frequently as formal ones ; at UVA, for example, the administration has held 16 hearings since 1998, as compared to 10 informal meetings.

And these proceedings can turn out positively for student victims. In January 2005, Carrie Ressler, then a junior at Concordia University, near Chicago, reported being raped by a football player after attending a party in his dorm. On January 19, within hours of the alleged assault, the police arrested the student athlete; by October, he'd pled guilty to battery for "knowingly [making] physical contact of an insulting nature," court records show.

At Concordia, Ressler's report landed on the desk of Dean of Students Jeffrey Hynes. The morning of the arrest, the dean summoned her to his office. "He told me he'd be telling the perpetrator he needed to leave by choice," she remembers Hynes saying. "If not, he'd be expelled." Within days, the athlete had left Concordia. Hynes declined to comment on Ressler's case.

"The dean acted in my interests," Ressler says. She recognizes, though, that the informal adjudication served the university's interests, too. "I got the sense from the dean that the school wanted to keep this case hush-hush."

Many victim advocates share Ressler's opinion on this. Often, these victim advocates charge, informal proceedings serve to sweep campus assaults under the rug. Both the Justice Department and the Education Department explicitly say in guidance documents that schools should not encourage mediation in sexual assault cases. Yet Katherine Lawson, an attorney at the Victim Rights Law Center, in Boston, says she's heard one local administrator boast they haven't held a full sexual assault hearing in years. "This meant to us that they had managed to pressure students to drop a complaint, mediate, or take some lesser administrative route," she explains, which kept cases quiet. At times, these proceedings even leave the victim advocates in the dark. Says one crisis-services coordinator at a Massachusetts university, "I don't have any idea what goes on in those little [deans'] meetings."

College Hearings: Little Transparency

More formal proceedings are sometimes no less shrouded. College disciplinary hearings, unlike courts, lack the trappings of transparency—campus spectators. Advocates can't attend unless serving as "advisers" to students. Only integral participants like board members or administrators have any clue when a hearing occurs. "They're secret *because* they're closed," says S. Daniel Carter, of Security on Campus Inc., a watchdog group.

Administrators see it differently, arguing that there are important distinctions between "secrecy" and "privacy." They can't open up internal proceeding—formal or informal—because that would amount to granting access to private educational records, which FERPA prohibits, they say. But that doesn't mean they're operating in secret. "Not providing private information to the rest of the world is respecting confidentiality and respecting FERPA as a law," says Mary Beth Mackin, assistant dean of student life at the University of Wisconsin-Whitewater. And while proceedings remain hidden to outsiders, administrators maintain they're conducted so students feel they're as open as possible.

Lisa Simpson would probably disagree. Her allegations of rape at the University of Colorado at Boulder blew open a scandal of sexual assault allegations against football players and recruits in 2004; three years later, her Title IX lawsuit brought against CU ended in a $2.85 million settlement in her favor. Yet she found

CU's judicial process a mystery. In December 2001, Simpson, then a CU sophomore, alleged she was raped by five football players and recruits during a beer-soaked party. They claimed she was a willing participant. Within days, Simpson's rape report made its way to CU's judicial affairs director, Matthew Lopez-Phillips. During a meeting in his office, she recalls him relaying how a panel of students, faculty, and staff would adjudicate. At the time, CU's official conduct code stated that alleged victims would generally be expected to participate in the process by "providing testimony at the formal hearing of the accused," among other things.

But Simpson never appeared before a panel. No panelist interviewed her about the report, or the victim impact statement she filed. Even after her five-year legal battle against CU over its response to her case—a battle that sparked a broader investigation, as well as systematic reform—she has no idea what transpired before the panel, or if it actually even existed. CU documents obtained by the Center show one accused student underwent a formal hearing as a result of Simpson's report; three others had informal, administrative proceedings. But some CU documents on the panel remain sealed by protective order, and only one includes a list of 17 possible panelists. Court records have revealed the identity of only one panelist. "For all I know," Simpson says, "it could have been a panel of athletic coaches."

Lopez-Phillips, who now works at Sonoma State University, did not respond to several calls and e-mails from the Center. Meanwhile, the sole panelist named in court records, Carlos Garcia, who directs CU's student center, declined to comment, citing "confidential" board sessions.

Adjudicating the Russell Case

Russell's proceedings before the UVA Sexual Assault Board commenced on May 10, 2004. According to the hearing transcript, Sisson, the board chair and senior associate dean, said: "All parties are reminded these proceedings are confidential ..."

It had become a familiar refrain for Russell. Before Russell filed her complaint, UVA deans spelled out the policy. In a March 1 e-mail, Rue told Russell:

It is perfectly okay to discuss the events that occurred with anyone you trust, but the fact that they are subject to a judicial proceeding through the university must be kept entirely confidential.

Reminders followed—in e-mails and letters stamped "CONFIDENTIAL." By the time the hearing occurred, Russell had heard the stipulation so often she refused to share documents with her mother. Over nine hours, as family and friends waited outside, the four-member board sat in a secured conference room, listening to testimony. Russell and the alleged assailant agreed on initial details—they ran into each other at a bar; he ended up at her dorm; she offered him an air mattress to sleep. But they painted different pictures of what transpired next. The man, Russell said, grabbed her from behind, ignored her pleas to stop, and "used [me] for his sexual need." Russell, the man countered, "tacitly agreed to have sex," demanding a condom, and never saying no. "Not all my actions would in a day-to-day situation be considered kosher," he wrote in his April 23, 2004 defense. "But none of my actions broached or even swept near the arena of rape."

Sisson repeated the confidentiality admonition 11 times during the hearing, according to the transcript. By its end, she relayed a directive that would wipe away much of the hearing record. "Leave all of your materials," she told participants, "so these materials are shredded."

Russell's mother, Susan, who had created a website criticizing UVA's response to campus rape allegations, claims Sisson admonished her, too, threatening to bring Kathryn up on disciplinary charges if the hearing verdict was posted on the site.

In a brief phone call with the Center, Sisson, now retired, described the proceedings as "entirely confidential at the time," and "a complicated set of circumstances." She said, "I approached my work and every one of these cases with the greatest professional integrity." Asked if She warned Russell not to talk or threatened disciplinary charges, she replied, "I cannot comment on specifics."

Going after Gag Orders

UVA administrators insist the confidentiality policy laid out in the school's 2004 written procedures was never meant to muzzle students, although they recognize students could "over interpret" its language. Nor was it official practice to warn them to keep quiet—or else. "There was no quid pro quo here that I know," says Nicole Eramo, current chair of the UVA Sexual Assault Board. "That was just not part of our policy." The actual written policy suggests otherwise—both old and new procedures state punishable actions "may include … violations of the rules of confidentiality." But administrators stress students have never gotten in trouble for telling their stories.

Instead, they blame their former policy on a longstanding confusion within higher education over the scope of FERPA in sexual assault proceedings. For decades, college administrators had operated under the assumption that FERPA protects all disciplinary proceedings—until the Clery Act passed in 1992. The Clery Act makes it mandatory for schools to notify alleged victims of hearing results. Understanding how FERPA intersects with Clery—two laws seemingly at odds—has been, in Eramo's words, "difficult for administrators."

That confusion, according to Carter, who heads public policy at Security on Campus Inc. has caused a proliferation of disturbing practices. Some schools have threatened alleged victims with expulsion for disclosing verdicts. Others have barred them from viewing their proceeding records. Still others have required confidentiality pacts—all citing FERPA. The Education Department found that institutions had even kept alleged victims in the dark. In September 2005, the department fined Miami University of Ohio $27,500 for breaking a promise to regulators to provide accurate written information about hearing results to student victims, as it had done to accused students. Earlier that year, in

June, the department determined that California State University, East Bay, had violated Title IX by not notifying alleged victims of the outcomes of sexual harassment investigations—requiring the school fix its policy under a resolution agreement.

By October 2002, Carter had petitioned the Department of Education about these sorts of practices. Alleged victims should be allowed to disclose not just the hearing results, he said, but also names of accused students and any sanctions. In March 2003, he filed a separate complaint against Georgetown University, which had been using gag orders in its proceedings. Like UVA, the Georgetown administration restricted students from divulging outcomes. Unlike UVA, it refused to release those outcomes unless students signed confidentiality agreements. Carter saw the pacts as clear violations of the Clery Act, which provides that "both the accuser and the accused shall be informed of the outcome of any campus disciplinary proceeding brought alleging a sexual assault."

In July 2004, the department agreed, issuing a ruling against Georgetown for its "impermissible non-disclosure agreement for Clery Act purposes." It ruled that Clery grants alleged victims a right to their proceeding outcomes, without restrictions, despite FERPA. Its final determination letter, dated July 16, required Georgetown to "discontinue its use of non-disclosure agreements."

Carter then went after illegal gag orders elsewhere—like one presented to Alphia Morin at the University of Central Florida. Now a former student, Morin found the school's process "very hidden to me" after filing a rape complaint against a scholarship athlete. In January 2005, the then-freshman learned she could only participate in the hearing before UCF's Student Conduct Board as a "witness" to her alleged assault. Save for her 20-minute testimony, the board banned her from the room. Later, she learned she could only receive the verdict by signing a confidentiality agreement.

Morin went public with her predicament in the campus newspaper, prompting Carter of Security on Campus Inc. to send a cautionary e-mail to UCF President John Hitt, warning that UCF's policy sounded illegal. Four days later, UCF sent Morin a copy of the verdict, with no written pacts attached. Carter managed to nullify verbal gag orders at schools including the College of William and Mary, among others, though he and administrators agree that written gag orders have always been pretty rare.

A Ruling against UVA

Kathryn Russell didn't think much about her school's policy until things went badly. At the hearing, board members asked questions making her wonder about their training—"Did it occur to you to perhaps leave the room?" "Why not just shut the door [on him]?" Sources familiar with the UVA board's training describe it as extensive; in 2004, the school required members to undergo a day of preparation featuring a videotape and reading materials, as well as sessions with outside experts on campus sexual assault. One previous board member describes Russell's panelists as open-minded and thoughtful. But the panel also judged her complaint using a "clear and convincing" evidence standard, which the Education Department ruled, in one 2004 case, is higher than Title IX authorizes—and which victim advocates argue is illegal.

In the end, the student Russell accused was found "not responsible" for sexual assault. The board instead slapped him with a verbal reprimand. "We ... believe that you used very bad judgment," Sisson declared. The case resulted in one of nine "not-responsible" verdicts the UVA board has handed down over the past decade, as compared to seven responsible ones.

"You can have a bad sexual experience but not be sexually assaulted under the university's definition and standard of evidence," says the prior UVA board member.

Russell saw it differently. "It was just a charade," she said.

In light of all those warnings about confidentiality, Russell thought she could tell no one what happened. But in November 2004, her mother filed a complaint against UVA with the Education Department, alleging violations under the Clery Act. It centered on the verbal threats of punishment, as did a second complaint filed on behalf of another former UVA student, Annie Hylton.

Hylton told the Center she had feared repercussions from UVA for going public in the local press that same month, even though her hearing dated to 2002.

"That's one reason I decided to go public," She relays. "If they were keeping me quiet, who else were they trying to keep quiet?"

In its official response, according to case records and a written statement from the Education Department, UVA argued it wasn't violating Clery so much as upholding FERPA and limiting what it termed "improper re-disclosures." Officials contended they could enforce the confidentiality policy through "pre-conditions" like a verbal commitment. While defending its policy, UVA was also reviewing the 2004 procedures. By March 2005, UVA administrators had submitted to the department a revamped policy that would soften the language and eliminate specific secrecy requirements. The new policy says the university "neither encourages nor discourages further disclosure."

In November 2008, however, the Education Department determined the school had violated the Clery Act. In a letter to UVA President John Casteen, it stated "the University cannot require an accuser to agree to abide by its non-disclosure policy, in writing or otherwise." The November 3, 2008 letter added:

It is … clear that several UVA students were persuaded that failure to adhere to the confidentiality policy could have resulted in serious consequences ranging from disciplinary action to not being granted a hearing before the Sexual Assault Board in the first place.

The department's UVA decision has made it clear that alleged student victims are no longer required to keep quiet about their hearing results. This year, in fact, the Education Department has amended its FERPA regulations to specify as much. The new regulations have thus effectively ended confidentiality requirements for hearing *results* on college campuses. But they have left open questions about broader secrecy requirements to *participate* in the college judicial process—even on the UVA campus.

Discretion or Lack of Accountability?

Inside the stately, red-brick Rotunda at UVA, administrators say the Education Department's decision represents the byproduct of a confused legal environment. And they assert that the school had already changed its confidentiality policy by the time the department issued its ruling. Unlike before, they say, the school's current procedures make plain that students can divulge their proceeding results, including accused students' names and any sanctions. The school has also taken steps to improve the process: it has bolstered investigations of rape allegations; improved training for the assault board; and added a lesser charge of "sexual misconduct" to its standards of conduct. Susan Davis, assistant vice president for student affairs, says UVA has "struck a good balance now." Indeed, deans elsewhere have touted the current UVA procedures as a national model.

But procedures at many schools, including UVA, still stipulate a confidential process—in formal hearings, and in informal mediations. For instance, UVA administrators still caution students not to discuss their proceedings during the process. Today's written procedures still specify that all proceeding "documents, testimony, or other evidence … may not be disclosed." Read the actual policy, and the only confidentiality language that has changed is the stipulation that students can divulge their proceeding results. But even that comes with a warning to, as the procedures state, "consult with legal counsel before doing so." To critics, the silencing effect of the old confidentiality rules still holds. But to UVA deans—and their colleagues elsewhere—there is legitimacy to ensuring a closed process as it unfolds. Some officials, such as UVA's Lampkin, insist a confidential procedure encourages reluctant alleged victims to come forward in the first place—a sentiment reinforced by some survey respondents. Others consider it crucial to ensure rights of accused students. Still others argue there is no need for outsiders to know details of campus rape proceedings because schools are deciding if a student's conduct violated institutional rules—not criminal laws.

"I've yet to hear students say they want a public process," says Davis.

"It's a balance between figuring out how to give students a safe space," Lampkin adds, "and having an environment where both the accuser and accused will come forward."

But critics say that attitude fails to acknowledge a fundamental flaw in the college judicial system: Without outside scrutiny, it lacks accountability. "The reason for disclosure and public oversight is that we can't allow educational institutions to police themselves," observes Mark Goodman, former head of the Student Press Law Center, which has pushed for more transparency. He, like many critics, believes the institutional reliance on confidentiality does more to protect the image of colleges than the anonymity of students. "I have a fundamental disagreement with schools over the notion that justice can be reached in secrecy," he says.

Controversy over Mediation

Not without unintended consequences, at least. In November 2003, Mallory Shear-Heyman, then a sophomore at Bucknell University in Pennsylvania, underwent a confidential mediation after reporting being raped in her dorm by a fellow student. Mediations became popular in disciplinary matters involving sexual assault earlier in the decade, and remain common today—despite controversy. In 2001, the Education Department deemed mediations improper partly because they carry no punishment. And while mediation is generally considered effective for resolving interpersonal conflicts, the department—and many critics—argue that it falls short in instances of sexual violence. The reason: an intimidating element exists between victims and their assailants because, like other serious assault, sexual assault is a violent act. "In some cases," the department states in its guidance document, referring to sexual assault cases, "mediation will not be appropriate even on a voluntary basis."

But Bucknell administrators defend their use of the practice, which they now call "voluntary facilitated dialogue," precisely because it only occurs at the request of an accusing student, with the willing participation of an accused student. Any power imbalance, they argue, is evened out by the presence of two administrators—one male, one female—guiding the conversation and assuring a comfortable setting. "Our students have really been key spokespeople for indicating they want some sort of option to have this dialogue," says Kari Conrad, judicial administrator for sexual misconduct. "We feel confident in keeping this process as a responsible response."

Shear-Heyman remembers Bucknell officials portraying the off-the-record session as an attractive way to confront the accused student, "as if it were the best option ever." Confidentiality, they relayed, would allow for more open and honest discussion. She was presented with a waiver, which specified that "information first disclosed during mediation may not be used in any subsequent internal University proceeding."

But Shear-Heyman wouldn't grasp the waiver's implications until the accused student, she says, implicated himself. Bucknell records show the student apologized to her in instant messages, admitting "b/c you got hurt, yes," what had occurred was rape. She says he repeated the admissions before the two deans who participated in the mediation—Gerald Commerford and Amy Badal. The waiver did not prevent Shear-Heyman from pursuing outside remedies. But the deans, she says, gave her the strong impression that she couldn't use what had occurred in the session— on or off campus. When she later considered pursuing criminal charges, she says, the deans claimed not to remember the accused student's alleged admissions.

Both Commerford and Badal told the Center they don't remember details from Shear-Heyman's mediation, including possible incriminating statements. And they claim not to recall her later asking them to corroborate such statements. "I don't recall any such scenario," says Badal.

Bucknell administrators insist it is standard practice to inform participants verbally and in writing that pursuing mediation won't preclude them from filing charges—on or off campus. Commerford describes himself and Badal as "sticklers about following the protocol." "I cannot speak for Mallory and her interpretations," he adds, "but I can tell you that we followed the protocol to a T."

One former Bucknell employee familiar with Shear-Heyman's mediation finds the practice "a problem because alleged assailants can say whatever they want without any repercussions"—a criticism voiced by many victim advocates. Bucknell University officials confirm that they wouldn't take action against an accused student who apologizes or confesses in mediation unless the victim were to file charges first—something that Shear-Heyman found pretty pointless. "After I'd realized how much I got screwed with the confidentiality," she says, "I didn't want to pursue anything further with the university." The former employee adds, "I absolutely think the practice serves the interest of the university, not the victims."

As for Russell, her life unraveled in the years after her proceeding at UVA. She lost weight, moved home, and divorced herself from friends. For years, she would find herself replaying in her mind, endlessly, details of her proceeding. She's long struggled to reconcile the fact that what she endured in pursuing a complaint had been for naught. Nothing had happened to her alleged assailant. "He was barely inconvenienced by having to attend the hearing," she says. Three years ago, Russell filed a civil lawsuit against him in Circuit Court for the City of Charlottesville, laying out her story in a complaint. The suit was never served on the man and eventually was dismissed at Russell's request, because, she says, she could not afford an attorney. The injustice of seeing her alleged assailant go unpunished has been, in her words, "the worst thing imaginable."

More recently, Russell discovered that the same student faced a second rape complaint at UVA. In April 2005, nearly a year after Russell's hearing, Rebekah Hay, then a UVA junior, filed that complaint, which ended up before two assault boards because the accused appealed—the first board returned a verdict against him; the second did not. Hay remembers Dean Rue addressing the suspect's history when she had filed her complaint. "She said to me, 'I'm sorry to see this name come up again,'" Hay recalls.

UVA administrators—and the alleged assailant—have stayed silent on the specifics of this complaint. Hay has never spoken publicly about her UVA case—until now. After all, the confidentiality of those proceedings was emphasized at UVA, she says, "and repeated and repeated and repeated again."

12

Not Alone: Report from the White House Task Force to Protect Students from Sexual Assault

The White House Task Force to Protect Students from Sexual Assault

The White House Task Force to Protect Students from Sexual Assault was established by President Barack Obama through a Presidential Memorandum on January 22, 2014. The task force is cochaired by the Office of the Vice President and the White House Council on Women and Girls.

This excerpt from the White House Task Force report famously begins with the statistic that "one in five women is sexually assaulted in college." The report then sets forth a set of action steps and recommendations, including identifying the problem through campus surveys, preventing sexual assault by engaging men on campus, and effectively responding when a student reports a sexual assault. The task force concludes that improved transparency and increased enforcement is needed on campuses in order to effectively respond to sexual assault on campus. This report is an early step in a larger campaign, undertaken by organizations and universities in partnership with the federal government, to better address the problem of sexual violence on US campuses.

"Not Alone," prepared by the White House Task Force, April 2014.

Executive Summary

Why We Need to Act

One in five women is sexually assaulted in college. Most often, it's by someone she knows—and also most often, she does not report what happened. Many survivors are left feeling isolated, ashamed or to blame. Although it happens less often, men, too, are victims of these crimes.

The President created the Task Force to Protect Students From Sexual Assault to turn this tide. As the name of our new website—NotAlone.gov—indicates, we are here to tell sexual assault survivors that they are not alone. And we're also here to help schools live up to their obligation to protect students from sexual violence.

Over the last three months, we have had a national conversation with thousands of people who care about this issue. Today, we offer our first set of action steps and recommendations.

1. Identifying the Problem: Campus Climate Surveys

The first step in solving a problem is to name it and know the extent of it—and a campus climate survey is the best way to do that. We are providing schools with a toolkit to conduct a survey—and we urge schools to show they're serious about the problem by conducting the survey next year. The Justice Department, too, will partner with Rutgers University's Center on Violence Against Women and Children to pilot, evaluate and further refine the survey—and at the end of this trial period, we will explore legislative or administrative options to require schools to conduct a survey in 2016.

2. Preventing Sexual Assault—and Engaging Men

Prevention programs can change attitudes, behavior—and the culture. In addition to identifying a number of promising prevention strategies that schools can undertake now, we are also researching new ideas and solutions. But one thing we know for sure: we need to engage men as allies in this cause. Most men are not perpetrators—and when we empower men to step in when someone's in trouble, they become an important part of the solution.

As the President and Vice President's new Public Service Announcement puts it: if she doesn't consent—or can't consent—it's a crime. And if you see it happening, help her, don't blame her, speak up. We are also providing schools with links and information about how they can implement their own bystander intervention programs on campus.

3. Effectively Responding When a Student Is Sexually Assaulted

When one of its students is sexually assaulted, a school needs to have all the pieces of a plan in place. And that should include:

Someone a survivor can talk to in confidence
While many victims of sexual assault are ready to file a formal (or even public) complaint against an alleged offender right away—many others want time and privacy to sort through their next steps. For some, having a confidential place to go can mean the difference between getting help and staying silent.

Today, we are providing schools with a model reporting and confidentiality protocol—which, at its heart, aims to give survivors more control over the process. Victims who want their school to fully investigate an incident must be taken seriously—and know where to report. But for those who aren't quite ready, they need to have—and know about—places to go for confidential advice and support.

That means a school should make it clear, up front, who on campus can maintain a victim's confidence and who can't—so a victim can make an informed decision about where best to turn. A school's policy should also explain when it may need to override a confidentiality request (and pursue an alleged perpetrator) in order to help provide a safe campus for everyone. Our sample policy provides recommendations for how a school can strike that often difficult balance, while also being ever mindful of a survivor's well-being.

New guidance from the Department of Education also makes clear that on-campus counselors and advocates—like those who work or volunteer in sexual assault centers, victim advocacy offices, women's and health centers, as well as licensed and pastoral counselors—can talk to a survivor in confidence. In recent years, some schools have indicated that some of these counselors and advocates cannot maintain confidentiality. This new guidance clarifies that they can.

A comprehensive sexual misconduct policy

We are also providing a checklist for schools to use in drafting (or reevaluating) their own sexual misconduct policies. Although every school will need to tailor a policy to its own needs and circumstances, all schools should be sure to bring the key stakeholders—including students—to the table. Among other things, this checklist includes ideas a school could consider in deciding what is—or is not—consent to sexual activity. As we heard from many students, this can often be the essence of the matter—and a school community should work together to come up with a careful and considered understanding.

Trauma-informed training for school officials

Sexual assault is a unique crime: unlike other crimes, victims often blame themselves; the associated trauma can leave their memories fragmented; and insensitive or judgmental questions can compound a victim's distress. Starting this year, the Justice Department, through both its Center for Campus Public Safety and its Office on Violence Against Women, will develop trauma-informed training programs for school officials and campus and local law enforcement. The Department of Education's National Center on Safe and Supportive Learning Environments will do the same for campus health centers. This kind of training has multiple benefits: when survivors are treated with care and wisdom, they start trusting the system, and the strength of their accounts can better hold offenders accountable.

Better school disciplinary systems

Many sexual assault survivors are wary of their school's adjudication process—which can sometimes subject them to harsh and hurtful questioning (like about their prior sexual history) by students or staff unschooled in the dynamics of these crimes. Some schools are experimenting with new models—like having a single, trained investigator do the lion's share of the fact-finding—with very positive results. We need to learn more about these promising new ideas. And so starting this year, the Justice Department will begin assessing different models for investigating and adjudicating campus sexual assault cases with an eye toward identifying best practices.

The Department of Education's new guidance also urges some important improvements to many schools' current disciplinary processes: questions about the survivor's sexual history with anyone other than the alleged perpetrator should not be permitted; adjudicators should know that the mere fact of a previous consensual sexual relationship does not itself imply consent or preclude a finding of sexual violence; and the parties should not be allowed to personally cross-examine each other.

Partnerships with the community

Because students can be sexually assaulted at all hours of the day or night, emergency services should be available 24 hours a day, too. Other types of support can also be crucial—like longer-term therapies and advocates who can accompany survivors to medical and legal appointments. Many schools cannot themselves provide all these services, but in partnership with a local rape crisis center, they can. So, too, when both the college and the local police are simultaneously investigating a case (a criminal investigation does not relieve a school of its duty to itself investigate and respond), coordination can be crucial. So we are providing schools with a sample agreement they can use to partner with their local rape crisis center—and by June, we will provide a similar sample for forging a partnership with local law enforcement.

4. Increasing Transparency and Improving Enforcement

More transparency and information

The government is committed to making our enforcement efforts more transparent—and getting students and schools more resources to help bring an end to this violence. As part of this effort, we will post enforcement data on our new website—NotAlone.gov—and give students a roadmap for filing a complaint if they think their school has not lived up to its obligations.

Among many other things on the website, sexual assault survivors can also locate an array of services by typing in their zip codes, learn about their legal rights, see which colleges have had enforcement actions taken against them, get "plain English" definitions of some complicated legal terms and concepts; and find their states' privacy laws. Schools and advocates can access federal guidance, learn about relevant legislation, and review the best available evidence and research. We invite everyone to take a look.

Improved Enforcement

Today, the Department of Education's Office for Civil Rights (OCR) is releasing a 52-point guidance document that answers many frequently asked questions about a student's rights, and a school's obligations, under Title IX. Among many other topics, the new guidance clarifies that Title IX protects all students, regardless of their sexual orientation or gender identity, immigration status, or whether they have a disability. It also makes clear that students who report sexual violence have a right to expect their school to take steps to protect and support them, including while a school investigation is pending. The guidance also clarifies that recent amendments to the Clery Act do not alter a school's responsibility under Title IX to respond to and prevent sexual violence.

OCR is also strengthening its enforcement procedures in a number of ways—by, for example, instituting time limits on negotiating voluntary resolution agreements and making clear that schools should provide survivors with interim relief (like changing housing or class schedules) pending the outcome of an OCR investigation. And OCR will be more visible on campus during its investigations, so students can help give OCR a fuller picture about what's happening and how a school is responding.

The Departments of Education and Justice, which both enforce Title IX, have entered into an agreement to better coordinate their efforts—as have the two offices within the Department of Education charged with enforcing Title IX and the Clery Act.

Next Steps

This report is the first step in the Task Force's work. We will continue to work toward solutions, clarity, and better coordination. We will also review the various laws and regulations that address sexual violence for possible regulatory or statutory improvements, and seek new resources to enhance enforcement. Also, campus law enforcement officials have special expertise to offer—and they should be tapped to play a more central role. We will also consider how our recommendations apply to public elementary and secondary schools—and what more we can do to help there.

* * *

The Task Force thanks everyone who has offered their wisdom, stories, expertise, and experiences over the past 90 days. Although the problem is daunting and much of what we heard was heartbreaking, we are more committed than ever to helping bring an end to this violence.

Introduction

For too many of our nation's young people, college doesn't turn out the way it's supposed to.

One in five women is sexually assaulted while in college.[1] Most often, it happens her freshman or sophomore year.[2] In the great majority of cases (75-80%), she knows her attacker, whether as an acquaintance, classmate, friend or (ex)boyfriend.[3] Many are survivors of what's called "incapacitated assault": they are sexually abused while drugged, drunk, passed out, or otherwise incapacitated.[4] And although fewer and harder to gauge, college men, too, are victimized.[5]

The Administration is committed to turning this tide. The White House Task Force to Protect Students From Sexual Assault was established on January 22, 2014, with a mandate to strengthen federal enforcement efforts and provide schools with additional tools to help combat sexual assault on their campuses. Today, we are taking a series of initial steps to:

1. Identify the scope of the problem on college campuses;

2. Help prevent campus sexual assault;

1 Krebs, C.P., Lindquist, C.H., Warner, T.D., Fisher, B.S., & Martin, S.L. (2007). *The Campus Sexual Assault (CSA) Study*. Washington, DC: National Institute of Justice, U.S. Department of Justice.; Krebs, C.P., Lindquist, C.H., Warner, T.D., Fisher, B.S., & Martin, S.L. (2009). College Women's Experiences with Physically Forced, Alcohol- or Other Drug-Enabled, and Drug-Facilitated Sexual Assault Before and Since Entering College. *Journal of American College Health*, 57(6), 639-647.

2 Krebs et al., *The Campus Sexual Assault (CSA) Study*.

3 *Ibid.*

4 *Ibid.*; see also Kilpatrick, D.G., Resnick, H.S., Ruggiero, K.J., Conoscenti, L.M., & McCauley, J. (2007). *Drug Facilitated, Incapacitated, and Forcible Rape: A National Study*. Charleston, SC: Medical University of South Carolina, National Crime Victims Research & Treatment Center.

5 The *CSA Study* found that 6.1% of college males were victims of either attempted or completed sexual assault. Although many advocates prefer to use the term "survivor" to describe an individual who has been sexually assaulted, the term "victim" is also widely used. This document uses the terms interchangeably and always with respect for those who have been subjected to these crimes.

3. Help schools respond effectively when a student is assaulted; and

4. Improve, and make more transparent, the federal government's enforcement efforts.

As the Task Force recognized at the outset, campus sexual assault is a complicated, multidimensional problem with no easy or quick solutions. These initial recommendations do not purport to find or even identify all of them. Our work is not over.[6]

Our First Task: Listening

Many people are committed to solving this problem. To hear as many of their views as possible, the Task Force held 27 listening sessions (12 webinars and 15 in-person meetings) with stakeholders from across the country: we heard from survivors; student activists; faculty, staff and administrators from schools of all types; parents; alumni; national survivors' rights and education associations; local and campus-based service providers and advocates; law enforcement; civil rights activists; school general counsels; men's and women's groups; Greek organizations; athletes; and researchers and academics in the field. Thousands of people joined the conversation.

Not surprisingly, no one idea carried the day. But certain common themes did emerge. Many schools are making important strides and are searching in earnest for solutions. A new generation of student activists is effectively pressing for change, asking hard questions, and coming up with innovative ways to make our campuses safer.

Even so, many problems loom large. Prevention and education programs vary widely, with many doing neither well. And in all too many instances, survivors of sexual violence are not at the heart of an institution's response: they often do not have a safe,

6 This first Task Force report focuses on sexual assault at postsecondary institutions—such as colleges, universities, community colleges, graduate and professional schools, and trade schools—that receive federal financial assistance. Thus, our use of the term "schools" refers to these postsecondary institutions.

confidential place to turn after an assault, they haven't been told how the system works, and they often believe it is working against them. We heard from many who reached out for help or action, but were told they should just put the matter behind them.

Schools, for their part, are looking for guidance on their legal obligations and best practices to keep students safe. Many participants called on the federal government to improve and better coordinate our enforcement efforts, and to be more transparent. And there was another constant refrain: get men involved. Most men are not perpetrators—and when we empower men to speak up and intervene when someone's in trouble, they become an important part of the solution.

I. How Best to Identify the Problem: Campus Climate Surveys

When then-Senator Joe Biden wrote the Violence Against Women Act 20 years ago, he recognized a basic truth: no problem can be solved unless we name it and know the extent of it. That is especially true when it comes to campus sexual assault, which is chronically underreported: only 2% of incapacitated sexual assault survivors, and 13% of forcible rape survivors, report the crime to campus or local law enforcement.[7]

The reasons for non-reporting (whether to a school or to law enforcement) vary. Many survivors of acquaintance rape don't call what happened to them rape and often blame themselves. One report found that 40% of college survivors feared reprisal by the perpetrator.[8] Survivors also cite fear of treatment by authorities, not knowing how to report, lack of independent proof, and not wanting families or other students to find out what happened.[9] Still others don't report because they don't want to participate in a formal college adjudication process.[10]

7 Krebs et al., *The Campus Sexual Assault (CSA) Study.*
8 Sampson, Rana (2002). *Acquaintance Rape of College Students*; Washington, DC: Office of Community Oriented Policing Services, U.S. Department of Justice.
9 Krebs et al., *The Campus Sexual Assault (CSA) Study.*
10 *Ibid.*

For colleges and universities, breaking the cycle of violence poses a unique challenge. When a school tries to tackle the problem— by acknowledging it, drawing attention to it, and encouraging survivors to report—it can start to look like a dangerous place. On the flip side, when a school ignores the problem or discourages reporting (either actively or by treating survivors without care), it can look safer. Add to this the competition for top students or a coveted spot on a college rankings list—and a school might think it can outshine its neighbor by keeping its problem in the shadows. We have to change that dynamic.

Schools have to get credit for being honest—and for finding out what's really happening on campus. Reports to authorities, as we know, don't provide a fair measure of the problem. But a campus climate survey can. When done right, these surveys can gauge the prevalence of sexual assault on campus, test students' attitudes and awareness about the issue, and provide schools with an invaluable tool for crafting solutions. And so:

- **We are providing schools with a new toolkit for developing and conducting a climate survey.** This guide explains the methods for conducting an effective survey—and contains a set of evidence-based sample questions to get at the answers.

- **We call on colleges and universities to voluntarily conduct the survey next year.** Again, a school that is willing to get an accurate assessment of sexual assault on its campus is one that's taking the problem—and the solution—seriously. Researchers recommend that schools conduct the survey in the winter or spring semesters, rather than when students first arrive on campus in the fall. Rutgers University, with its leading research institute on violence against women,[11] will pilot and evaluate the survey. Also, the Justice Department's Office on Violence Against Women will work with its campus grantees to conduct the survey and evaluate it. And the Bureau of Justice Statistics will further refine the survey

---

11 The Center on Violence Against Women & Children at the School of Social Work.

methodology. What we learn from these pilots, evaluations, and schools' experiences will chart the path forward for everyone—and will culminate in a survey for all to use.

- **We will explore legislative or administrative options to require colleges and universities to conduct an evidence-based survey in 2016.** A mandate for schools to periodically conduct a climate survey will change the national dynamic: with a better picture of what's really happening on campus, schools will be able to more effectively tackle the problem and measure the success of their efforts.

II. Preventing Sexual Assault on Campus

Participants in our listening sessions roundly urged the Task Force to make prevention a top priority. Some even suggested that if prevention and education efforts don't start earlier, it's too late by the time students get to college. While we certainly agree that this work should begin early, the college years, too, are formative. During this transition to adulthood, attitudes and behaviors are created or reinforced by peer groups. And students look to coaches, professors, administrators, and other campus leaders to set the tone. If we get this right, today's students will leave college knowing that sexual assault is simply unacceptable. And that, in itself, can create a sea change.

Federal law now requires schools to provide sexual assault prevention and awareness programs.[12] To help colleges and universities in this endeavor, we are providing schools with new guidance and tools.

- **Best practices for better prevention.** The Centers for Disease Control and Prevention (CDC) conducted a systematic review

12 *See* 20 U.S.C. § 1092(f) (The Jeanne Clery Disclosure of Campus Security and Campus Crimes Statistics Act, commonly known as the Clery Act). The Department of Education is currently engaged in negotiated rule-making to implement the VAWA 2013 amendments to the Clery Act that require schools to provide education and awareness programs and to improve their campus security policies. Rule-making is scheduled to be completed in 2015, but schools are expected to make a good faith effort now to meet the new requirements.

of primary prevention strategies for reducing sexual violence, and is releasing an advance summary of its findings. CDC's review summarizes some of the best available research in the area, and highlights evidence-based prevention strategies that work, some that are promising, and—importantly—those that don't work. The report points to steps colleges can take now to prevent sexual assault on their campuses.

- Among other things, CDC's review shows that effective programs are those that are sustained (not brief, one-shot educational programs), comprehensive, and address the root individual, relational and societal causes of sexual assault. It also includes a listing of prevention programs being used by colleges and universities across the country, so schools can better compare notes about effective and encouraging approaches.[13]
- **Getting everyone to step in: bystander intervention.** Among the most promising prevention strategies—and one we heard a lot about in our listening sessions—is bystander intervention. Social norms research reveals that men often misperceive what other men think about this issue: they overestimate their peers' acceptance of sexual assault and underestimate other men's willingness to intervene when a woman is in trouble.[14]

And when men think their peers don't object to abusive behavior, they are much less likely to step in and help. Programs like *Bringing in the Bystander*[15] work to change those perspectives—and teach men (and women) to speak out against rape myths (*e.g.*,

13 For a concise and complementary factsheet on prevention strategies, *see* http://notalone.gov/assets/preventionoverview.pdf.

14 Berkowitz, A.D. (2010). "Fostering Healthy Norms to Prevent Violence and Abuse: The Social Norms Approach." Accessed from: http://www.alanberkowitz.com/articles/Preventing%20Sexual%20Violence%20Chapter%20-%20Revision.pdf.

15 Banyard, V. L., Moynihan, M. M., & Plante, E. G. (2007). Sexual violence prevention through bystander education: An experimental evaluation. *Journal of Community Psychology*, 35, 463-481.

women who drink at parties are "asking for it") and to intervene if someone is at risk of being assaulted.

- **To help enlist men as allies, we are releasing a Public Service Announcement featuring President Obama, Vice President Biden, and celebrity actors.** The message of the PSA is simple: if she doesn't consent—or can't consent— it's a crime. And if you see it happening, help her, don't blame her, speak up. We particularly urge men's groups, Greek organizations, coaches, alumni associations, school officials and other leaders to use the PSA to start campus conversations about sexual assault.
- **To help keep these conversations going, we are providing a basic factsheet on bystander intervention.** In addition to the CDC summary, this document identifies the messages and skills that effective programs impart, describes the various ways to get the word out (in-person workshops, social marketing campaigns, online training, interactive theater) and provides links to some of the more promising programs out there.

[…]

III. Responding Effectively When a Student is Sexually Assaulted

Sexual assault is a crime—and while some survivors turn to the criminal justice system, others look to their schools for help or recourse. Under federal law, when a school knows or reasonably should know that one of its students has been sexually assaulted, it is obligated to act. These two systems serve different (though often overlapping) goals. The principal aim of the criminal system is to adjudicate a defendant's guilt and serve justice. A school's responsibility is broader: it is charged with providing a safe learning environment for all its students—and to give survivors the help they need to reclaim their educations. And that can mean a number of things—from giving a victim a confidential place to turn for advice and support, to effectively investigating and finding out what happened, to sanctioning the perpetrator, to doing everything we can to help a survivor recover. The Task Force is taking the following steps:

Giving Survivors More Control: Reporting and Confidentially Disclosing What Happened

Sexual assault survivors respond in different ways. Some are ready to make a formal complaint right away, and want their school to move swiftly to hold the perpetrator accountable.

Others, however, aren't so sure. Sexual assault can leave victims feeling powerless—and they need support from the beginning to regain a sense of control. Some, at least at first, don't want their assailant (or the assailant's friends, classmates, teammates or club members) to know they've reported what happened. But they do want someone on campus to talk to—and many want to talk in confidence, so they can sort through their options at their own pace. If victims don't have a confidential place to go, or think a school will launch a full-scale investigation against their wishes, many will stay silent.

In recent years, some schools have directed nearly all their employees (including those who typically offer confidential services, like rape crisis and women's centers) to report all the details of an incident to school officials—which can mean that a survivor quickly loses control over what happens next. That practice, however well-intentioned, leaves survivors with fewer places to turn.

This is, by far, the problem we heard most about in our listening sessions. To help solve it:

- **Schools should identify trained, confidential victim advocates who can provide emergency and ongoing support**. This is a key "best practice." The person a victim talks to first is often the most important. This person should understand the dynamics of sexual assault and the unique toll it can take on self-blaming or traumatized victims. The advocate should also be able to help get a victim needed resources and accommodations, explain how the school's grievance and disciplinary system works, and help navigate the process. As many advocates have learned over the years, after survivors receive initial, confidential support, they often decide to proceed with a formal complaint or cooperate in an investigation

- **We are also providing schools with a sample reporting and confidentiality protocol.** A school, of course, must make any policy its own—but a few guiding principles should universally apply. As noted, some sexual assault survivors are ready to press forward with a formal (or even public) complaint, while others need time and privacy to heal. There is no one-size-fits-all model of victim care. Instead, there must be options.

That means, at a minimum, that schools should make it clear, up front, who on campus will (or will not) share what information with whom. And a school's policy should also explain when it may need to override a request for confidentiality (and pursue an alleged perpetrator) in order to provide a safe campus for everyone. The watchword here is clarity: both confidential resources and formal reporting options should be well and widely publicized—so a victim can make an informed decision about where best to turn.

And in all cases, the school must respond. When a student wants the school to take action against an offender—or to change dorms or working arrangements—the school must take the allegation seriously, and not dissuade a report or otherwise keep the survivor's story under wraps. Where a survivor does not seek a full investigation, but just wants help to move on, the school needs to respond there, too. And because a school has a continuing obligation to address sexual violence campus-wide, it should always think about broader remedial action—like increasing education and prevention efforts (including to targeted groups), boosting security and surveillance at places where students have been sexually assaulted, and/or revisiting its policies and practices.

[…]

Training for School Officials

Sexual assault can be hard to understand. Some common victim responses (like not physically resisting or yelling for help) may seem counter-intuitive to those unfamiliar with sexual victimization. New research has also found that the trauma associated with rape or sexual assault can interfere with parts of the brain that control memory—and, as a result, a victim may have impaired verbal skills, short term memory loss, memory fragmentation, and delayed recall.[16] This can make understanding what happened challenging.

Personal biases also come into play. Insensitive or judgmental comments—or questions that focus on a victim's behavior (e.g., what she was wearing, her prior sexual history) rather than on the alleged perpetrator's—can compound a victim's distress.

Specialized training, thus, is crucial. School officials and investigators need to understand how sexual assault occurs, how it's perpetrated, and how victims might naturally respond both during and after an assault.

[…]

New Investigative and Adjudicative Protocols: Better Holding Offenders Accountable

Separate and apart from training, we also need to know more about what investigative and adjudicative *systems* work best on campus: that is, who should gather the evidence; who should make the determination whether a sexual assault occurred; who should decide the sanction; and what an appeals process, if the school has one, should look like.

---

16 Bremner, J.D., Elzinga, B., Schmahl, C., & Vermetten, E. (2008). Structural and functional plasticity of the human brain in posttraumatic stress disorder. *Progress in Brain Research.* 167(1), 171-186; Nixon, R. D., Nishith, P., & Resick, P. A. (2004). The Accumulative Effect of Trauma Exposure on Short-Term and Delayed Verbal Memory in a Treatment-Seeking Sample of Female Rape Victims. *Journal of Traumatic Stress,* 17(1), 31-35.

Schools are experimenting with new ideas. Some are adopting different variations on the "single investigator" model, where a trained investigator or investigators interview the complainant and alleged perpetrator, gather any physical evidence, interview available witnesses—and then either render a finding, present a recommendation, or even work out an acceptance-of-responsibility agreement with the offender. These models stand in contrast to the more traditional system, where a college hearing or judicial board hears a case (sometimes tracking the adversarial, evidence-gathering criminal justice model), makes a finding, and decides the sanction.

Preliminary reports from the field suggest that these innovative models, in which college judicial boards play a much more limited role, encourage reporting and bolster trust in the process, while at the same time safeguarding an alleged perpetrator's right to notice and to be heard.

[...]

13

Obama's Campus Sexual Assault Guidelines Are Problematic

Wendy Kaminer

Wendy Kaminer is a lawyer and a social critic who often writes on topics of feminism, law, and popular culture.

Wendy Kaminer has several concerns with "Not Alone," the White House task force's report on campus sexual assaults. One of her biggest concerns is the report's dictate to universities that "parties should not be allowed to cross-examine each other." According to Kaminer, this denies the accused party the fundamental right of a defense from his or her accuser, and traumatizes students who might be falsely accused. This is especially concerning given that racial and ethnic minorities are more likely to be accused of sexual assault than other groups. Kaminer concludes that "[e]very student accused of a crime or disciplinary infraction has an equal right to due process and fair adjudication of charges."

"Not Alone," the White House entitled its task force report on campus sexual assaults. "Believe the Victim," the report might as well have been called. It reflects a presumption of guilt in sexual assault cases that practically obliterates the due process rights of the accused. Students leveling accusations of assault are automatically described as "survivors" or "victims" (not alleged victims or complaining witnesses), implying that their accusations are true.

Excerpts from "Victimizing the Accused? Obama's Campus Sexual Assault Guidelines Raise Concerns," by Wendy Kaminer, WBUR.org, May 5, 2014.

When you categorically presume the good faith, infallible memories and entirely objective perspectives of self-identified victims, you dispense with the need for cumbersome judicial or quasi-judicial proceedings and an adversary model of justice. Thus the task force effectively prohibits cross-examination of complaining witnesses: "The parties should not be allowed to cross-examine each other," the report advises, denying the fundamental right to confront your accuser.

Alleged victims are supposed to be protected from "hurtful questioning." The impulse to protect actual victims from the ordeal of a cross-examination by their attackers is laudable. But by barring cross-examination, you also protect students who are mistaken or lying, and you victimize (even traumatize) students being falsely accused.

School officials are also encouraged to substitute a "single investigator" model for a hearing process, which seems a prescription for injustice. As the Foundation for Individual Rights in Education points out, pursuant to this model, "a sole administrator would be empowered to serve as detective, judge and jury, affording the accused no chance to challenge his or her accuser's testimony."

These "reforms" exacerbate an already dangerously unreliable approach to evaluating charges of assault. In 2011, the Department of Education issued guidelines requiring colleges and universities to employ a minimal "preponderance of evidence" standard in cases involving allegations of harassment or violence. This is the lowest possible standard of proof, which merely requires discerning a 50.01 percent chance that a charge is more likely than not to be true. It facilitates findings of guilt, which will be merited in some cases, and not others. For students wrongly accused, the consequences of a guilty finding can be as dire as a not guilty finding for students actually victimized.

These are difficult, potentially traumatizing cases for all parties involved, and not surprisingly some students complaining of sexual assault prefer not to participate in investigations or hearings. How do you evaluate their claims? If you're the White House task force, you simply presume that they're true: "Where a survivor does not seek a full investigation, but just wants help to move on, the school needs to respond there too." Move on from having "survived" precisely what? You can sympathize with a victimized student who doesn't want to pursue a claim and still wonder how school officials can respond fairly and intelligently to an accusation that hasn't been investigated and may or may not be true.

Does this approach exaggerate or trivialize the problem at hand? Sexual assault is a serious felony, the task force and victim advocates would agree. According to the Administration, one in five students are victimized by it. Assume that estimate is accurate and imagine that 20 percent of the people in a community are suffering violent assaults. Residents would likely demand a stronger police presence and stepped up criminal prosecutions, rather than informal neighborhood councils to "adjudicate" complaints. But on campus, felony complaints are to be prosecuted informally, the way schools might prosecute violations of a dress code, without affording accused students any meaningful rights.

Justifications for this include the particular ambiguities of sexual assault charges on campus. Alleged assaults often involve alcohol, actual victims may know their attackers and, in a closed campus community, may be hesitant to press accusations against them. The irony is that these factors complicating the prosecution of campus assaults and inspiring calls for informal, non-adversarial responses to them are the same factors that, as victim advocates rightly assert, have encouraged victim blaming and prevented law enforcement authorities from taking allegations of campus assaults seriously.

The solution to the problem of ignoring sexual assault charges shouldn't be assuming that they're true. The "believe the victim" biases underlying the White House task force report aren't subtle or inconsequential, but they're not generally recognized by left of center media. The occasional students' rights watchdog, like Brooklyn College professor KC Johnson, offers a critical, in depth analysis of the Administration's approach, but in general reactions are dictated by partisan or ideological biases: The right has its own politically correct mandate to oppose any Obama Administration civil rights initiative. The left labors under a pop feminist mandate to reflexively believe self-identified victims of sexual assault.

Similar assumptions about victimization often dictate how people view the rights of the accused and their accusers. Compare the administration's disregard for due process in formulating disciplinary procedures for campus sexual misconduct complaints to its critique of harsh, due process-less disciplinary practices in elementary and secondary schools.

School discipline tends to be discriminatory, at least in effect, targeting racial and ethnic minorities, so civil rights advocates outside the Administration are rallying against it, rightly seeking due process protections for students accused. But in response to allegations of sexual misconduct in colleges and universities, the same advocates generally favor a prosecutorial approach that sacrifices due process over protections for presumed victims.

How do we account for these opposing approaches to student rights? Considering elementary and secondary school disciplinary practices, the administration sympathizes with students accused. In campus sexual assault cases, it sympathizes with accusers. But rights shouldn't be allocated on the basis of subjective sympathies, unless we want to encourage discrimination—the sort of discrimination that plagues minority students in public schools. Every student accused of a crime or disciplinary infraction has an equal right to due process and fair adjudication of charges. You're also "Not Alone," the Administration should guarantee students accused of sexual assault. You're accompanied by fundamental rights.

14

Bystanders Can Help Prevent Campus Sexual Violence

Leyna Johnson

Leyna Johnson is a graduate of the State University of New York at Geneseo, where she presented this paper at the SUNY Geneseo GREAT Day Symposium.

In this academic study, Nicole Leyna Johnson investigates whether or not a person's gender makes them more likely to help a potential victim of party rape. Interviewing over 200 undergraduate students at a small liberal arts college, the author found that men "reported less intent to help, perceived more barriers to helping, and accepted more rape myths than women." Following these results, Johnson states that bystander education programs would be effective in teaching bystanders—and especially male bystanders—about the realities of sexual violence and how to prevent sexual assault. Bystanders can be an effective tool in sexual assault prevention on campuses.

Abstract

This study investigates the individual differences in bystander intent to help a potential victim of party rape. The potential victim was described as an intoxicated woman who was escorted by an apparently sober man into a back bedroom. Undergraduate students at a small liberal arts college (N = 209, 76.1% women) read the description and responded to measures of intent to help,

"Are Gender Differences in Bystander Intent to Help a Potential Victim of Party Rape Mediated by Barriers to Help, Rape Myth Acceptance, or Both?" by Leyna Johnson, ojs. geneseo.edu, https://ojs.geneseo.edu/index.php/great/article/view/1774/1220. Licensed under CC BY 3.0.

barriers to helping, and rape myth acceptance. As expected, intent to help correlated negatively with barriers to helping and rape myth acceptance. Also as expected, men reported less intent to help, perceived more barriers to helping, and accepted more rape myths than women. Multivariate analyses showed that the gender difference in intent to help was mediated by barriers to helping but not rape myth acceptance. Bystander education programs that explicitly address barriers to helping, including skills deficits and audience inhibition, may be more effective in engaging bystanders to prevent sexual assault.

Campus sexual assault is a common problem in the United States. Krebs, Lindquist, Warner, Fischer, and Martin (2007) found that 19% of college women experience completed or attempted sexual assault; cases define sexual assault as forced touching of a sexual nature, oral sex, sexual intercourse, anal sex, and/or sexual penetration with a finger or object. Party rape is a form of sexual assault that takes place either on or off campus; it typically involves plying the victim with alcoholic beverages to obtain sexual access (Armstrong, Hamilton, & Sweeney, 2006). Twenty percent of college women experience rape, and 72% of the rapes that occurred were attributed to alcohol intoxication (Mohler-Kuo, Dowdall, Koss, & Wechsler, 2004). A common occurrence on college campuses are pre-assault risks. Pre-assault risks are factors that can contribute to an increased likelihood of being a victim of sexual assault. These factors include being female and alone at a party, being female and with friends (male or female) at a party, intoxication of victim or perpetrator, being in a secluded or dark area, and males exhibiting "pre-rape behaviors" (Rozee & Koss, 2001, p. 299). Pre-rape behaviors include attitudes of sexual entitlement, exhibition of power and control, hostility, anger, and acceptance of interpersonal violence (Rozee & Koss, 2001).

Currently, campus sexual assault is being addressed by bystander educational programs that aim to prevent party rape and other forms of rape. A bystander is a witness to an emergency, crime, or other dangerous situations, but is not directly involved like a victim or perpetrator (Banyard & Moynihan, 2011). Bystander education is the approach to preventing campus sexual assault. By letting the community attempt to intervene and prevent situations within which a party rape might occur, the focus away from victims and perpetrators and encourages individuals in the community to take action (McMahon, 2010). The reduction of bystander inhibition is a major goal of bystander education programs.

Bystander inhibition can be experienced in multiple ways and at various stages of risk awareness. Intervention barriers are internal thoughts or beliefs that prevent a bystander from taking action to prevent party rape. Latané and Darley outlined five steps that need to be taken for a bystander to intervene (as cited in Burn, 2009). Each step has a separate but related barrier; the first step is to notice the event, the second step is to identify the event as intervention-appropriate, the third step is to take responsibility, the fourth step is to decide how to help, and the fifth step is to act to intervene. Burn (2009) found that individuals who experienced greater barriers to helping offered less help in situations of possible party rape within a hypothetical survey. In another hypothetical survey by Bennett, Banyard, and Garnhart (2014), failure to take responsibility and inadequate skills were the most prevalent barriers tied to sexual assault situations. It may be expected that bystanders who experience more barriers will help to female victims of party rape.

Although many situational factors have potential to influence barriers in bystander-helping behavior, personal attitudes on the part of the bystander could also inhibit the act of helping. Rape myths are defined as a complex set of cultural beliefs that lead to the perpetuation of male sexual violence against women (Payne, Lonsway, & Fitzgerald, 1999). Rape myths can affect the perspective of potential bystanders with regard to possibly risky situations, which can in turn affect bystander helping behavior. In a survey of attitudes towards sexual assault, McMahon (2010) found that individuals who accept rape myths more readily were less likely to intervene in potential rape situations than individuals with lower acceptance of rape myths. It may be expected that bystanders with higher rates of rape myth acceptance are less likely than bystanders with lower rates of rape myth acceptance to offer help to female victims of party rape.

Bystander inhibition may be affected by the social group of the victim in relation to the bystander. Social categorization theory suggests that individuals view others in their social group (in-group) more favorably than those outside their social group (outgroup). Although social groups tend to have negative associations such as diffusion of responsibility, there are also positive associations such as social cohesion and co-operation (Turner, Hogg, Oakes, Reicher, & Wetherell, 1987). Consequently, maintaining a positive view of in group members could create a sense of duty in bystanders and influence them to intervene, an act which would lower bystander inhibition rates. The Levine, Cassidy, Brazier, and Reicher (2002) study was an analogue study in which participants watched a video of a man being attacked. The participants were asked whether or not they would provide help to the man in question; fellow student participants in the same social category were more likely to offer help than participants who were not in the same social category.

Gender is a type of social group. Women may be less likely than men to participate in bystander inhibition and therefore more likely to offer help to a female student at risk for party rape due to their shared gender group. There are mixed results in the literature. The Banyard and Moynihan (2011) study was a retrospective study in which participants were asked about sexual assault in general; women bystanders were found to offer more help than men bystanders. In a longitudinal study of sexual assault attitudes, Banyard (2008) found that women were more likely than men to offer help in situations of sexual assault. However, in an analogue study conducted by Fischer, Greitemeyer, Pollozek, and Frey (2006), participants witnessed a woman being harassed by a physically threatening male or a non-physically threatening male and no gender difference in helping behavior was found. Another analogue study conducted by Levine et al. (2002) found no gender differences in bystander-helping behavior. The lack of gender difference in these two studies may be due to the fact that the studies were based upon physical assault rather than sexual assault.

Some research suggests that men would rather appear to be masculine to other men and the fear of appearing weak is be the reason that men are less likely to help women in rape situations. (Carlson, 2008). An analogue study conducted by Tice and Baumeister (1985) found that when participants heard a potential choking victim, masculine individuals offered less help than other participants. In a hypothetical study where students in an introductory psychology class were asked to answer questions on sexual assault prevention attitudes, opinions, and behaviors, Burn (2009) found that men experience higher numbers of barriers (other than inhibition due to a skills deficit) as bystanders in a pre-assault stage than women. Men give less concrete intervention strategies than do women (Koelsch, Brown, & Boisen, 2012). Because men experience more inhibitions than women, women's offer of help to female victims should be higher. It may be expected that women bystanders are more likely than men bystanders to offer help to a female at risk for party rape.

However, gender differences in rape myth acceptance have been found more consistently. Eyssel, Bohner, and Siebler (2006) found that men who believe they're in a group that has higher rates of rape myth acceptance report higher amounts of rape proclivity. When men perceive their peers as accepting of rape myths, they are more inclined to perpetrate behaviors than intervene. Hinck and Thomas (1999) found that although college students tend to disagree with rape myths in general, men tend to disagree less with rape myths. McMahon (2010) found that men have greater rates of rape myth acceptance than women. A multicultural study found similar results in regards to gender, but determined that American students have higher rape myth acceptance than Scottish students (Muir & Payne, 1996); this difference could be due to American culture promoting higher rape myth acceptance. Further research is needed to understand gender differences in rape myth acceptance, especially in America.

The following study was conducted in order to investigate factors that influence bystander responses to risk for party rape. The first hypothesis stated that bystanders who experience greater barriers to helping will offer less help to victims at risk for party rape.

This difference could be due to barriers causing bystander inhibition (Burn, 2009). The second hypothesis was that bystanders who have higher rates of rape myth acceptance will offer less help to victims at risk for party rape. This difference may be due to the acceptance of rape myths inhibiting bystander behavior (McMahon, 2010). The third hypothesis was that men bystanders will experience more barriers than women bystanders, based on research conducted by Burn (2009). The fourth hypothesis was that men bystanders may be more likely than women bystanders to accept rape myths. The fifth hypothesis was that men bystanders might be less likely than women bystanders to offer help to a female at risk for party rape and the sixth hypothesis was that these differences may be due to men experiencing more barriers to helping and accepting more rape myths than women. The current study adds to the literature by building off past retrospective studies on rape myth acceptance and looking at bystander helping behavior offered in an analogue situation (McMahon, 2010). The current study also adds to the limited research on barriers by building off of Burn's (2009) study and by looking at an analogue situation to determine whether bystanders with higher barriers would offer less help.

Method

Participants
Data was collected from 209 undergraduates (76.1% female) at a small public college in Western N.Y. The mean age of participants was 19.20 (SD = 1.36), and ranged from 17 to 26. Eighty-five

students (40.7%) were freshman, 62 students (29.7%) were sophomores, 41 students (19.6%) were juniors, and 21 students (10.0%) were seniors. One hundred and seventy-two participants (82.3%) responded as White/ Caucasian, 14 participants responded as Asian or Asian American (6.7%), 12 participants (5.7%) responded as Black/African American, 10 participants (4.8%) responded as Hispanic/Latino/Chicano, and one participant (0.5%) responded as Native American.

Design

A multivariate correlational design was used within which one between-subjects variable (bystander gender; men and women) was compared to two different sets of dependent variable causes of bystander inhibition (rape myth acceptance and barriers to help) and intent to offer direct help.

Measures

Intent to help. Six bystander helping responses were adapted from Chabot, Tracy, Manning, and Poisson (2009), as well as Levine and Crowther (2008) in the present study. Six direct helping methods (e.g., "ask the drunk girl if she is okay") were assessed to create a scale for direct help. A Likert-type scale was used to determine how likely it was that participants would enact a behavior (1 = *strongly disagree*, 7 = *strongly agree*). Scores were averaged; higher scores indicated greater intent to offer direct help. Reliability of this measure was demonstrated in past research by Katz, Colbert, and Colangelo (2015). Internal consistency was found to be good in the present study ($\alpha = .90$).

Barriers to helping. Nine questions with regards to four of the barriers to bystander intervention behavior were adapted from Burn (2009) in the present study. One item from the risk identification barrier was "stay out of it, given no one else seems concerned." Five items were from the failure to take responsibility barrier which was "leave it up to others to get involved." One item from the skills deficit barrier was "know what to say or do in this situation." Two items from the audience inhibition barrier were "worry that if you got involved, you might look stupid" and "decide not to get involved because unsure if others will support you." A Likert-type scale was used to determine how likely it was that participants would experience each barrier (1 = *definitely likely*, 7= *definitely unlikely*). Scores were averaged and higher scores indicated greater experience of barriers. The author demonstrated the reliability of this measure. In the current study, the estimate of internal consistency was found to be good ($\alpha = .85$).

Rape myth acceptance. The Illinois Rape Myth Acceptance Short Form (IRMA-SF) was designed to assess participant's agreement with various rape myths and was used in the current study (Payne et al., 1999). The IRMA-SF is composed of 17 items (e.g., "when women are raped, it's often because the way they said "no" was ambiguous"). A Likert-type scale was used to determine how likely participants were to accept rape myths (1 = *strongly disagree*, 5 = *strongly agree*). Scores were averaged with higher scores indicating greater acceptance of rape myths. The authors provided evidence for the reliability of this measure. Internal consistency in the present study was found to be good ($\alpha = .86$).

Procedure

From an online database provided by the psychology department studies, undergraduate students participated, voluntarily, in a study that dealt with *Attitudes and Reactions of Different Party Safety Messages and Situations*. All participants provided informed consent. Participants filled out surveys in classrooms on campus. Participants were instructed to imagine that they were at a party where they witnessed an intoxicated woman being led into a private bedroom by a seemingly sober man. Participants answered their reaction to the event as well as some personal characteristics on a self-reported scale. Data collection sessions lasted for no longer than an hour. When participants completed their surveys they placed the papers in a slotted box. Participants received extra credit from class as compensation. Full disclosures were provided.

Results

Overall, participants were somewhat likely to offer direct help to potential victims of party rape (M = 4.95, SD = 1.58, ranging from 1 to 7). Participants experienced a moderate amount of barriers (M = 3.27, SD = 1.21, ranging from 1 to 6.63). Rape myth acceptance was low (M = 1.62, SD = 0.50, ranging from 1 to 3.18).

Hypothesis one was that participants who experienced higher numbers of barriers were less likely to provide direct help to a potential victim of party rape than participants who experienced lower numbers of barriers. A negative correlation was found between the number of barriers experienced and the amount of direct help offered to potential victims in the first hypothesis, r (207) = -.67, p < .001. Similarly, hypothesis two stated that there would be a negative correlation between rape myth acceptance and direct help offered to potential victims, r (206) = -.21, p < .01. Again, the second hypothesis was supported by the study.

Hypothesis three and four stated that there would be bystander gender differences in barriers to help as well as rape myth acceptance. Two independent sample t-tests were conducted to examine gender differences in barriers to helping and rape myth acceptance.

There also was a significant between-groups difference in barriers, t (206) = -2.63, p < .009. As expected, men bystanders were significantly more likely to experience barriers (M = 3.66, SD = 1.14) than women bystanders (M = 3.15, SD = 1.21). Hypothesis three was supported. There was a significant, between-groups, difference in rape myth acceptance, t (64.21) = -4.61, p < .001. As expected, men bystanders were more likely to accept rape myths (M = 1.94, SD = 0.60) than women bystanders (M = 1.52, SD = 0.41). The fourth hypothesis was supported.

Regression analyses were conducted to examine whether barriers to helping and rape myth acceptance might account for expected gender differences in helping. In the first regression, the gender of the bystander predicted direct help (β = .15, p <.05); full model F (1, 205) = 4.77, p < .05. This suggested significant gender differences in direct helping behavior, supporting hypothesis 5. In a second regression, barriers to help (β = -.65, p <.001) and rape myth acceptance (β = -.06, ns) were added to the model, F (3, 203) = 54.08, p < .001. The significant β, for barriers to help but not rape myth acceptance, suggests that barriers to help explain gender differences more accurately because bystander gender was no longer a significant predictor in the second model (β = .01, ns). The sixth hypothesis was partially supported.

Discussion

The purpose of this study was to investigate factors that influence bystander helping behavior in order to help prevent potential party rape. As expected, bystanders who reported more barriers and higher rates of rape myth acceptance were less likely to offer direct help to a potential victim at risk for party rape than bystanders with lower numbers of barriers and rates of rape myth acceptance. Also as expected, men reported more barriers and higher rates of rape myth acceptance than women. Finally, as expected, men bystanders were less likely to offer help than women bystanders; this gender difference was found to result from barriers to help rather than rape myth acceptance.

The presented study found that, generally, bystanders who have more barriers offer less help than bystanders who have fewer barriers. This finding was similar to Burn's (2009) research, and expands on this research by looking at barriers experienced by bystanders within an analogue situation of party rape. The present study also found that bystanders who accept higher numbers of rape myths offer less direct help than bystanders who accept fewer rape myths. The current results were similar to McMahon's (2010) older results and builds off this research by looking at situations of party rape instead of sexual assault in general, and by using an analogue design as opposed to a retrospective design.

The present study found that men bystanders experienced more barriers to help than women bystanders. The current findings were, again, similar to findings from Burn (2009). The present study found that men bystanders accept more rape myths than women bystanders. The current findings were similar to past results (Muir & Payne, 1996; McMahon, 2010). The present study replicates past findings of gender differences in barriers to help and rape myth acceptance.

The current study found that men bystanders offer less help to potential victims of party rape than women bystanders. The present findings were similar to Banyard (2008) and Levine and Crowther (2008), but differ from Fischer et al. (2006). The current study extends Banyard's (2008) study of sexual assault attitudes by specifically looking at situations of party rape in an analogue design instead of a longitudinal design. The present paper also builds off Levine and Crowther's (2008) study by looking at female victims of potential party rape, not physical violence. In an unambiguous situation of harassment, Fischer et al.'s (2006) study showed no gender differences in helping behavior, but the current study found that gender differences affect helping behavior in an ambiguous situation of party rape.

The present study found that gender differences in bystander help could be attributed to barriers to helping but not rape myth acceptance. Banyard (2008) found that there are gender differences in bystander helping in situations of sexual assault but no potential explanations were explored. The current study expands on Banyard's (2008) study by exploring possible explanations of gender differences in bystander help. Consistent with Burn (2009), the present study found that the more barriers to help that bystanders were presented with, the less likely they were to offer direct help to potential victims of party rape, and that men bystanders experienced more barriers to help than women bystanders. The present study extended past research by showing that gender differences in barriers to help could account for gender differences in direct helping behavior. In contrast to past research, the current study found that to the degree that bystanders accepted more rape myths, they offered less direct help to potential victims of party rape, and rape myth acceptance was higher in men bystanders than women bystanders. However, rape myth acceptance did not explain the gender differences in bystander help offered to potential victims of party rape beyond the direct effect of barriers. Rape myth acceptance could be related to barriers to helping, as shown by a secondary analysis, r (206) = .22, p < .001, which suggests that rape myth acceptance may affect barriers, and barriers, in turn, explain gender differences in helping behavior. The current study does not explain gender differences in helping as they to rape myth acceptance beyond barriers to help.

Despite the significant findings of the current study, there were limitations. Some limitations to the current study involved participant variability (or lack of), only female victims being represented, and only two possible explanatory factors of bystander inhibition. Most of the participants in the present study were women, and the underrepresentation of men could misrepresent the actual helping behavior in the general population. Multiple studies have found no gender differences in helping behavior (Fischer et al., 2006; Banyard & Moynihan, 2011). Participants predominantly identified as Caucasian in the present study. Although it has been found that party rape is a problem typically associated with individuals who identify as white (Armstrong et al., 2006), having the perspective of a more well-rounded sample might generalize better. The present study only looked at the differences of gender, barriers to help, and rape myth acceptance, when other possible sources of bystander inhibition exist, such as victim blame or empathy, and social status of the victim in relation to the bystander.

The current study found that gender differences in helping behavior could be attributed to barriers to help. However, due to the design of the study, the first barrier, "notice the event," could not be tested. An analogue study could be conducted to include this barrier in testing in order to see whether that specific barrier also has gender differences. Bennett et al. (2014) found that if participants were to notice an event as a pre-assault risk, they would be more likely to intervene. The present study found that overall rape myth acceptance was low and did not contribute to gender differences in bystander helping behavior, but could be linked to barriers to help. Further research could be conducted to examine this link and the role it plays in bystander intervention. For example, a correlational study could be conducted to see which barriers are affected by rape myth acceptance. Other factors of bystander helping behavior should be researched. For example, do bystanders offer more or less help based on the race or age of the victim? When does a potentially ambiguous situation like the pre-assault risk condition become less ambiguous to potential bystanders? Researchers should focus on which situations promote bystander helping behavior in party rape situations. The current study as well as many past studies (Bennett et al., 2014; Levine et al., 2002) have looked at the relationship between the bystander and the victim in helping behavior. Burn (2009) found that men were likely to intervene when the perpetrator was a friend, but the research did not look at women bystander intervention with perpetrators. Further research can lead to the founding of better bystander education programs which, in turn, could lead to more intervention on behalf of individuals at risk for party rape within the community.

The present study has wide-reaching applications. Krebs et al. (2007) found that one in five college women are victims of sexual assault or attempted sexual assault. The current approach to preventing these crimes is the establishment of bystander intervention programs on college campuses. The current study explores some possible explanations that can be attributed to bystander helping behavior. Further research is necessary to fully understand situations that lead to bystander helping behavior.

References

Armstrong, E. A., Hamilton, L., & Sweeney, B. (2006). Sexual assault on campus: A multilevel, integrative approach to party rape. *Social Problems, 53*(4), 483-499. doi:10.1525/sp.2006.53.4.483

Banyard, V. L. (2008). Measurement and correlates of prosocial bystander behavior: The case of interpersonal violence. *Violence and Victims, 23*(1), 83-97. doi:10.1891/0886-6708.23.1.83

Banyard, V. L., & Moynihan, M. M. (2011). Variation in bystander behavior related to sexual and intimate partner violence prevention: Correlates in a sample of college students. *Psychology of Violence, 1*(4), 287-301. doi:10.1037/a0023544

Bennett. S., Banyard, V. M., & Garnhart, L. (2014). To act or not to act, that is the question? Barriers and facilitators of bystander intervention. *Journal of Interpersonal Violence, 29*(3), 476-496. doi:10.1177/0886260513505210

Burn, S. M. (2009). A situational model of sexual assault prevention through bystander intervention. *Sex Roles, 60,* 779-792. doi:10.1007/s11199-008-9581-5

Carlson, M. (2008). I'd rather go along and be considered a man: Masculinity and bystander intervention. *The Journal of Men's Studies, 16*(1), 3-17. doi:10.3149/jms.1601.3

Chabot, H. F., Tracy, T. L., Manning, C. A., & Poisson, C. A. (2009). Sex, attribution, and severity influence intervention decisions of informal helpers in domestic violence. *Interpersonal Violence, 24*(10), 1696-1713. doi:10.1177/0886260509331514

Eyssel, F., Bohner, G., & Siebler, F. (2006). Perceived rape myth acceptance of others predicts rape proclivity: Social norm or judgmental anchoring? *Swiss Journal of Psychology/Schweizerische Zeitschrift Für Psychologie/Revue Suisse De Psychologie, 65*(2), 93-99. doi:10.1024/1421-0185.65.2.93

Fischer, P., Greitemeyer, T., Pollozek, F., & Frey, D. (2006). The unresponsive bystander: Are bystanders more responsive in dangerous emergencies? *European Journal of Social Psychology, 36*(2), 267-278. doi:10.1002/ ejsp.297

Hinck, S. S., & Thomas, R. W. (1999). Rape myth acceptance in college students: How far have we come? *Sex Roles, 40*(9), 815-832.

Katz, J., Colbert, S., & Colangelo, L. (2015). Effects of group status and victim sex on female bystanders' responses to a potential party rape. *Violence and Victims, 30*(2), 265-278. doi:10.1891/0886-6708.VV-D-13-00099

Koelsch, L. E., Brown, A. L., & Boisen, L. (2012). Bystander perceptions: Implications for university sexual assault prevention programs. *Violence and Victims, 27*(4), 563-79. doi:10.1891/0886-6708.27.4.563

Krebs, C. P., Lindquist, C. H., Warner, T. D., Fisher, B. S., & Martin, S. L. (2007). *The campus sexual assault (CSA) study: Final Report.* Retrieved from https://www.ncjrs.gov/pdffiles1/ nij/ grants/221153.pdf

Latane, B., & Darley, J. M. (1970). *The unresponsive bystander: Why doesn't he help?* New York, NY: Appleton-Century-Crofts.

Levine, M., Cassidy, C., Brazier, G., & Reicher, S. (2002). Self-categorization and bystander non-intervention. *Journal of Applied Social Psychology, 32*(7), 1452-1463. doi:10.1111/j.1559-1816.2002.tb01446.x

Levine, M., & Crowther, S. (2008). The responsive bystander: How social group membership and group size encourage as well as inhibit bystander intervention. *Journal of Personality and Social Psychology, 95*(6), 1429-1439. doi:10.1037/ a0012634

McMahon, S. (2010). Rape myth beliefs and bystander attitudes among incoming college students. *Journal of American College Health, 59*(1), 3-11. doi:10.1080/07448481.2010.483 715

Mohler-Kuo, M., Dowdall, G. W., Koss, M. P., & Wechsler, H. (2004). Correlates of rape while intoxicated in a national sample of college women. *Journal of Studies on Alcohol, 65*(1), 37-45. doi:10.15288/jsa.2004.65.37

Muir, G., Lonsway, K. A., & Payne, D. L. (1996). Rape myth acceptance among Scottish and American students. *The Journal of Social Psychology, 136*(2), 261-262. doi:10.1080/0022 4545.1996.9714002

Payne, D. L., Lonsway, K. A., & Fitzgerald, L. F. (1999). Rape myth acceptance: Exploration of its structure and its measurement using the Illinois rape myth acceptance scale. *Journal of Research in Personality, 33*(1), 27-68. doi:10.1006/jrpe.1998.2238

Rozee, P. D., & Koss, M. P. (2001). Rape: A century of resistance. *Psychology of Women Quarterly, 25*(4), 295-311. doi:10.1111/1471-6402.00030

Tice, D. M., & Baumeister, R. F. (1985). Masculinity inhibits helping in emergencies: Personality does predict the bystander effect.

Journal of Personality and Social Psychology, 49(2), 420-428. doi:10.1037/0022-3514.49.2.420

Turner, J. C., Hogg, M. A., Oakes, P. J., Reicher, S. D., & Wetherell, M. S. (1987). A selfcategorization theory. *Rediscovering the social group: A self-categorization theory* (pp. 42-67). Oxford, UK: Basil Blackwell Ltd.

Organizations to Contact

The editors have compiled the following list of organizations concerned with the issues debated in this book. The descriptions are derived from materials provided by the organizations. All have publications or information available for interested readers. The list was compiled on the date of publication of the present volume; the information provided here may change. Be aware that many organizations take several weeks or longer to respond to inquiries, so allow as much time as possible.

Arte Sana
PO Box 1334
Dripping Springs, TX 78620
(512) 858-4069
email: artesanando@yahoo.com
website: http://www.arte-sana.com

Meaning "art heals" in Spanish, Arte Sana is an advocacy group for Latinas in the United States who have experienced sexual assault. Its bilingual website provides local resources across the United States, educational resources, and information about advocacy.

Black Women's Blueprint Project
PO Box 23713
Brooklyn, NY 11202
(347) 533-9102
email: info@blackwomensblueprint.org
website: http://www.blackwomensblueprint.org

Black Women's Blueprint is a human rights organization that has done important work in addressing sexual violence against African American women. The project's Black Women's Truth and Reconciliation Commission (BWTRC) documents sexual abuse against women of African descent in the United States and provides healing symposia across the United States.

Canadian Association of Sexual Assault Centres (CASAC)
(604) 876-2622
email: casac01@shaw.ca
website: http://www.casac.ca

Canada's only organization of sexual assault centers has come together to educate Canadians about sexual violence and provide resources to local sexual assault centers. CASAC has built alliances with other groups in order to promote women's equality and anti-sexual violence.

Joyful Heart Foundation
32 West 22nd Street
New York, NY 10010
(212) 475.2026
email: info@joyfulheartfoundation.org
website: http://www.joyfulheartfoundation.org

Actress Mariska Hargitay founded Joyful Heart in 2004 in order to help sexual assault survivors heal and reclaim the joy in their lives. The foundation carries out its mission through education, advocacy, and healing programs designed to help survivors of sexual assault.

Loveisrespect
(866) 331-9474
website: http://www.loveisrespect.org

Loveisrespect is a 24-hour web and telephone resource for teenagers and young adults who have experienced sexual abuse. Created with the help of the Office on Violence Against Women of the United States Department of Justice, those in need of help following a sexual assault can live chat, text, or call the hotline to connect with trained peer advocates.

MaleSurvivor
4768 Broadway, #527
New York, NY 10034
(941) 720-7062
email: tmassa@malesurvivor.org
website: http://www.malesurvivor.org

MaleSurvivor emerged after the first Conference on Male Sexual Victimization in 1988. Since then, MaleSurvivor has been a leading organization fighting for the rights of male victims of sexual abuse. The organization began providing Weekends of Recovery to support survivors and their loved ones in 2001 and has helped over 1,000 survivors since then.

Men Can Stop Rape
1130 6th Street NW, Suite 100
Washington, DC 20001
(202) 265-6530
email: info@mencanstoprape.org
website: http://www.mencanstoprape.org

Men Can Stop Rape is dedicated to mobilizing men and boys to prevent violence and sexual violence against women. The organization provides workshops and prevention programs to teach men how to stop sexual violence, including bystander intervention.

National Alliance to End Sexual Violence (NAESV)
1129 20th Street NW, Suite 801
Washington, DC 20036
email: info@endsexualviolence.org
website: http://www.endsexualviolence.org

The National Alliance to End Sexual Violence is a coalition of statewide anti-sexual violence organizations formed to provide a voice in Washington to advocate against sexual violence and for survivors. Its team publishes analysis of legal trends in regard to sexual violence legislation, arranges media interviews, and advises members of Congress.

National Sexual Violence Resource Center (NSVRC)
123 North Enola Drive
Enola, PA 17025
(717) 909-0710
email: resources@nsvrc.org
website: http://www.nsvrc.org

The National Sexual Violence Resource Center was founded to prevent and respond to sexual violence through providing educational resources, research, and references for direct services to sexual assault survivors. While the NSVRC does not provide counseling or health services itself, it can connect survivors with local programs.

Rape, Abuse, and Incest National Network (RAINN)
1220 L Street NW, Suite 505
Washington, DC 20005
National Sexual Assault Hotline: (800) 656-4673
email: info@rainn.org
website: http://www.rainn.org
online chat: online.rainn.org

RAINN is the largest anti-sexual violence organization in the United States. It operates a 24/7 hotline and online chat for those who need help following a sexual attack. RAINN also provides educational programming on preventing sexual violence and helping survivors of sexual attacks.

Bibliography

Books

Annie E. Clark and Andrea L. Pino. *We Believe You: Survivors of Campus Sexual Assault Speak Out.* New York, NY: Holt Paperbacks, 2016.

Kirby Dick and Amy Ziering. *The Hunting Ground: The Inside Story of Sexual Assault on American College Campuses.* New York, NY: Hot Books, 2016.

Lauren J. Germain. *Campus Sexual Assault: College Women Respond.* New York, NY: Routledge, 2015.

Alison E. Hatch. *Campus Sexual Assault: A Reference Handbook.* Santa Barbara, CA: ABC-CLIO, 2017.

Monika Korra. *Kill the Silence: A Survivor's Life Reclaimed.* New York, NY: Harmony, 2015.

Jon Krakauer. *Missoula: Rape and the Justice System in a College Town.* New York, NY: Doubleday, 2015.

Wendy McElroy. *Rape Culture Hyseria: Fixing the Damage Done to Men and Women.* CreateSpace, 2016.

Kelly Oliver. *Hunting Girls: Sexual Violence from The Hunger Games to Campus Rape.* New York, NY: Columbia University Press, 2016.

Michele A. Paludi. *Campus Action Against Sexual Assault: Needs, Policies, Procedures, and Training Programs.* Westport, CT: Praeger, 2016.

Samuel R. Staley and Ruth Krug. *Unsafe on Any Campus?: College Sexual Assault and What We Can Do About It.* Tallahassee, FL: Southern Yellow Pine Publishing, 2016.

US Senate Subcommittee on Financial and Contracting Oversight. *Sexual Violence on Campus: How Too Many Institutions of Higher Education Are Failing to Protect Students.* CreateSpace, 2015.

Robert Uttaro. *To The Survivors: One Man's Journey as a Rape Crisis Counselor with True Stories of Sexual Violence.* CreateSpace, 2013.

Michael P. Watts. *Sexual Violence on Campus: Overview, Issues, and Actions.* Hauppauge, NY: Nova Science, 2015.

Sara Carrigan Wooten and Roland W. Mitchell. *The Crisis of Campus Sexual Violence: Critical Perspectives on Prevention and Response.* Baltimore, MD: Johns Hopkins University Press, 2016.

Sara Carrigan Wooten and Roland W. Mitchell. *Preventing Sexual Violence on Campus: Challenging Traditional Approaches Through Program Innovation.* New York, NY: Routledge, 2016.

Periodicals and Internet Sources

Tyler Bishop, "The Laws Targeting Campus Rape Culture," *The Atlantic*, September 11, 2015. http://www.theatlantic.com/ education/archive/2015/09/the-laws-targeting-campus-rape -culture/404824.

Jena Nicols Curtis and Susan Burnett, "The Role of EMS in Helping Survivors of Campus Sexual Violence," *Journal of Emergency Medical Services*, April 5, 2015. http://www.jems.com/articles/ print/volume-41/issue-40/features/the-role-of-ems-in-helping -survivors-of-campus-sexual-violence.html.

Jennifer J. Freyd, "Official Campus Statistics for Sexual Violence Mislead," *Al Jazeera*, July 14, 2014. http://america.aljazeera.com/ opinions/2014/7/college-campus-sexualassaultsafetydatawhiteho usegender.html.

Beth Howard, "How Colleges Are Battling Sexual Violence," *US News*, August 28, 2015. http://www.usnews.com/news/ articles/2015/08/28/how-colleges-are-battling-sexual-violence.

Huffington Post Contributors, "Breaking the Silence: Addressing Sexual Assault on Campus," *Huffington Post*, 2016. http://www .huffingtonpost.com/news/breaking-the-silence.

Christopher P. Krebs, et al., "The Campus Sexual Assault (CSA) Study," US Department of Justice, December 2007. https://www .ncjrs.gov/pdffiles1/nij/grants/221153.pdf.

Abbie Nehring, "Campus Sexual Assault: What Are Colleges Doing Wrong?," *ProPublica*, July 29, 2014. https://www.propublica.org/ article/campus-sexual-assault-what-are-colleges-doing-wrong.

NPR Editors, "A Closer Look at Sexual Assaults on Campus," *NPR*, 2014. http://www.npr.org/series/339884470/a-closer-look-at -sexual-assaults-on-campus.

Richard Pérez-Peña, "1 in 4 Women Experience Sex Assault on Campus," *New York Times*, September 21, 2015. http://www

.nytimes.com/2015/09/22/us/a-third-of-college-women
-experience-unwanted-sexual-contact-study-finds.html.

Lauren R. Taylor and Jessica Raven, "Alcohol Isn't the Cause of
Campus Sexual Assault. Men Are," *Washington Post*, June
10, 2016. https://www.washingtonpost.com/posteverything/
wp/2016/06/10/alcohol-isnt-what-causes-campus-sexual-assault
-men-are.

Jacquelyn White, "Confronting Campus Sexual Violence," *Psychology
Today*, November 16, 2015. https://www.psychologytoday.com/
blog/sound-science-sound-policy/201511/confronting-campus
-sexual-violence.

The White House Task Force to Protect Students from Sexual Assault,
"Preventing Sexual Violence on College Campuses: Lessons from
Research and Practice," Not Alone, April 2014. https://notalone
.gov/assets/evidence-based-strategies-for-the-prevention-of-sv
-perpetration.pdf.

Alia Wong, "Why the Prevalence of Campus Sexual Assault Is SO
Hard to Quantify," *The Atlantic,* January 26, 2016. http://www
.theatlantic.com/education/archive/2016/01/why-the-prevalence
-of-campus-sexual-assault-is-so-hard-to-quantify/427002.

Marcia G. Yerman, "Campus SaVE Act Responds to College
Campus Sexual Violence," *Huffington Post*, July 29, 2015. http://
www.huffingtonpost.com/marcia-g-yerman/campus-save-act-
responds-_b_7868236.html.

Emily Yoffe, "The College Rape Overcorrection," *Slate,* December 7,
2014. http://www.slate.com/articles/double_x/doublex/2014/12/
college_rape_campus_sexual_assault_is_a_serious_problem_
but_the_efforts.html.

Index